At Issue

Is the U.S. Ready for a Minority President?

Other Books in the At Issue Series:

At Issue

Is the U.S. Ready for a Minority President?

Amanda Hiber, Book Editor

GREENHAVEN PRESS

An imprint of Thomson Gale, a part of The Thomson Corporation

Detroit • New York • San Francisco • New Haven, Conn. • Waterville, Maine • London

Christine Nasso, *Publisher*
Elizabeth Des Chenes, *Managing Editor*

© 2008 The Gale Group.

Star logo is a trademark and Gale and Greenhaven Press are registered trademarks used herein under license.

For more information, contact:
Greenhaven Press
27500 Drake Rd.
Farmington Hills, MI 48331-3535
Or you can visit our Internet site at http://www.gale.com

Articles in Greenhaven Press anthologies are often edited for length to meet page require-ments. In addition, original titles of these works are changed to clearly present the main thesis and to explicitly indicate the author's opinion. Every effort is made to ensure that Greenhaven Press accurately reflects the original intent of the authors. Every effort has been made to trace the owners of copyrighted material.

LIBRARY OF CONGRESS CATALOGING-IN-PUBLICATION DATA

Is the U.S. ready for a minority president? / Amanda Hiber, book editor.
    p. cm. -- (At issue)
    Includes bibliographical references and index.
    ISBN-13: 978-0-7377-3878-0 (hardcover)
    ISBN-13: 978-0-7377-3879-7 (pbk.)
    1. Presidents--United States--Election. 2. Minorities--United States--Political activity.
    I. Hiber, Amanda. II. Is the United States ready for a minority president? III. Series.
    JK528.I8 2007
    324.973--dc22
                                                                    2007032272

ISBN-10: 0-7377-3878-2 (hardcover)
ISBN-10: 0-7377-3879-0 (pbk.)

Printed in the United States of America
10 9 8 7 6 5 4 3 2 1

Contents

Introduction

In America's 232-year history, it has elected a strikingly homogenous pool of presidents. These forty-two individuals have all been Caucasian Christian men—in fact, all but one have been Protestant. While women and members of ethnic, racial, and religious minority groups have made tremendous gains in election to public office, including both houses of Congress, they have yet to even come close to winning the White House. In 1972, Shirley Chisholm became the first African American to seek a major party's nomination for president. Before her run for this office, she'd been the first African American woman elected to Congress. To date, a major party has never nominated a woman or minority to the nation's highest office.

America's lack of progress in presidential elections is even more evident when compared to other countries, many of which are widely seen as less socially advanced than the U.S. For instance, worldwide, thirty-six women have been elected to lead their countries, including Britain, Ireland, Germany, Iceland, India, Israel, and Nicaragua. As Vicki Haddock writes in the *San Francisco Chronicle*, "Even Pakistan, where women in some regions are forbidden to leave their homes without a male escort, is among the forty-two countries that have had at least one woman as president or prime minister over the last half century." Indeed, it is puzzling that a country at the forefront of the feminist movement of the 1960s and 1970s, with legislation that treats women far more equally to men than many countries, has still not elected a woman to lead it.

It is equally puzzling that a country known for providing opportunity for all has only elected white men as presidents. This fact seems to stand in stark contradiction to a Constitution that asserts, "All men are created equal" and promises "Liberty and Justice for all." More recently, America is known for the advances it has made in the wake of the Civil Rights Movement, such as desegregation, the banning of employment and housing discrimination, and the restoration of voting rights. Yet as Jeremy I. Levitt writes in the *Chicago Sun-Times*, "The hard reality is that whether Democrat or Republican, white voters generally do not support black candidates." White voters' apparent refusal to elect a minority seems to call into question how far America has actually come since the blatantly discriminatory practices of the 1960s and earlier. Is America really rid of prejudice and discrimination if minorities and women are still, in effect, being excluded from the presidency?

At the same time, many social commentators point to a number of tangible explanations for America's failure to elect women and minorities to the presidency. Michael Hill writes in the *Baltimore Sun* that, unlike European countries where voting rights were determined by class, in the U.S., "First voting rights were given to white males, then, after the Civil War, to black males. Women were the only ones excluded." Another reason the U.S. has been slow to elect a woman president is that in the U.S., politics have been closely associated with traditionally masculine qualities. Haddock writes that in America:

> The role of commander in chief conjures up a "warrior image"—one favoring traditional masculinity instead of political instincts that seem more maternal.
>
> What's more, the peculiarities of our American character make it harder for female contenders. In our movie idols and our presidents, Americans value rugged individualism, bravado, a cowboy mystique—a role that men find easier to play.

One explanation for the lack of women and minorities in the Oval Office that cannot be ignored is that there have simply been far fewer *candidates* from these groups. Beyond this, Haddock points out that there is a "lack of women in the political pipeline. The United States ranks 68th among the world's countries in terms of our ratio of female representatives in the national legislature, according to the Inter-Parliamentary Union." Indeed, while women make up 51 percent of the U.S. population, they make up only 16 percent of the 110th Congress. The same can be said for racial, ethnic, and religious minority groups. Of the 535 members of the 110th Congress, only seventy-five are African American, Asian American, or Hispanic American. Thus, these three groups make up at least 26 percent of the U.S. population yet roughly 14 percent of Congress. Hill attributes America's lack of women and minority presidents to "the inertia built into the American political system." He continues:

> In countries with parliamentary systems and numerous political parties, many different kinds of candidates can emerge, different genders, different ethnicities, different political beliefs.

> But in the United States, only two get to run. That makes it difficult for any unrepresented group—women, blacks, Hispanics or Green Party believers—to get to the top of the political food chain.

It seems that the series of events that led America to elect forty-two Caucasian Christian men may amount to something more complicated than mere sexism or racism.

Against this historic backdrop, the 2008 presidential election promises to be a landmark one, with a black man, Senator Barack Obama, and a woman, Senator Hillary Clinton, vying for the Democratic nomination. In addition, Mormon Mitt Romney and Mexican American Governor Bill Richardson have announced their candidacies. Only time will tell the outcome of the next election, but one thing is for sure: This is the closest the U.S. has come to electing either a woman or a minority president. In *At Issue: Is the U.S. Ready for a Minority President?* the authors discuss what obstacles, if any, stand in the way of the U.S. electing a woman or minority. With the 2008 presidential campaign already in full swing, the question of whom the American people will or will not elect to lead them is critical to the future of the country.

1

The U.S. Is Ready for a President Who Is Not a White Male

Ellen Goodman

Ellen Goodman writes a column for the Boston Globe *that appears in more than 375 newspapers. She was awarded the Pulitzer Prize for Distinguished Commentary in 1980.*

Discussion of the 2008 presidential election has already begun and in particular, many analysts are asking whether America is ready for a president who is not a white male. This issue poses the familiar question of whether changes in social attitudes lead to political change, or vice versa. Nevertheless, America is finally able to see presidential candidates as individuals and not as representatives of their race or gender. Polls show that Americans themselves are ready for a non-white-male president but are less hopeful that the rest of the country feels similarly. It may only be this cynicism that stands in the way of electing a minority or female president in 2008.

Maybe it wasn't such a great Christmas gift after all. The baseball caps, emblazoned with the last day of the [George W.] Bush presidency—Jan. 19, 2009—seemed to offer my favorite Democratic couple a light at the end of the tunnel. But sometimes it's easier to see the tunnel than the light.

Nevertheless, January is about to mark the earliest opening for any presidential campaign in memory. So allow me to end the old year and begin the new by taking a look at the question dominating the news magazines and talk shows: Is America ready for a president who isn't a white male?

The only Democrats who so far have actually announced their candidacies are indeed white and male, from Tom Vilsack to John Edwards. But the sexier and racier question dominating the early chatter is the possible mano-a-womano, black-and-white matchup that could be offered with Hillary Rodham Clinton or Barack Hussein Obama atop the national ticket.

Ready? Political readiness is not exactly like reading readiness. For generations, strategists and psychologists have posed the same chicken-and-egg riddle for social change. Do you need a change in attitudes before you can succeed in changing real life? Or does a change in reality produce a change in attitudes?

The answer is, of course, yes.

Having lived through enormous change, having seen people resist change, adjust, and then protect and promote one new "status quo" after another, I think we operate with too much fear about "readiness" and too much pessimism about backlash.

For the first time in history, a female candidate is the most experienced, the most ready-on-Day-One option for the Oval Office.

I sometimes think we have two very different national attitudes toward the pace of technological change and the pace of political change. It's as if we were all eager, early adopters when it comes to iPods, and late adopters when it comes to presidents.

Reasons for Hope

As we turn to 2007 and 2008, I don't think we have to be cockeyed optimists to believe that Americans can get beyond seeing "a female" and "a black" to seeing a candidate.

Consider Massachusetts, where a Mormon Republican white man is being followed into the governor's office by an African American Democratic man who defeated a white Republican woman. Was Massachusetts "ready" for "a" Mormon before Mitt Romney? Was it ready for "an" African-American before Deval Patrick?

Let's take the briefest stock of the individual strengths and weaknesses of the two way-too-early frontrunners in the Democratic Party. There is no doubt that Democrats have developed a crush on Obama, a man of thoughtful charm, relaxed intelligence, and ineffable authenticity. The reservations against him are that he's unknown, untested, and "young." (Memo to the baby-boomer media dubbing him as young: No, you were not young at 45.)

Whether that crush becomes a commitment depends on how his "authenticity" survives delivering a stump speech 14 times a day under a Jon Stewart watchdog. And how resilient he is after the inevitable YouTube moment.

As for Hillary? If Barack is the new boy on the block, Hillary is the smarter, sadder-but-wiser gal. For the first time in history, a female candidate is the most experienced, the most ready-on-Day-One option for the Oval Office.

Yet the reservations about her have to do with her baggage, her husband, and her haters. Hillary's success will depend perversely on whether she can convince those Democrats who would vote for her that others will, too. Her election depends on being seen as "electable."

I don't dismiss racism and sexism in these equations. I watched the campaign ads against Harold Ford Jr. in Tennessee [when Ford, a Democrat, ran for Senate against Republican Bob Corker, the Republican Party ran a television ad widely denounced as racist], I heard Rahm Emanuel [Democratic member of the House of Representatives] ask, "What the (expletive) happened to my women?," when only three of 17 Democratic women candidates challenging Republicans for congressional seats won. But Clinton and Obama are individuals with very personal stories. Not class actions.

America's Self-Perception

In *Newsweek*, 93 percent of Americans said they would vote for an African-American for president, but only 56 percent believed that the country is ready for one. Similarly, 86 percent said they would vote for a woman, but only 55 percent believed the country was ready for one.

Traditionally, if cynically, we assume that the lower figure is the one that matters, the real one. But maybe that gap between us and them—open-minded us and close-minded them—doesn't grow out of an inflated view of ourselves but a deflated view of our country.

Is the country ready? Almost all Americans believe or want to believe that they would vote for a president without prejudice. That's either an agent for change or an indicator of change. If we believe we vote for the person, not the race or the gender, maybe we will. 2007, 2008. Ready—or not—here we go.

2

The U.S. Is More Ready for a Black President than a Woman President

Benjamin Wallace-Wells

Benjamin Wallace-Wells is a contributing editor of The Washington Monthly. *His work has also appeared in* The Boston Globe, The New Yorker, Rolling Stone *and* Policy Review.

The fact that two of the frontrunners for the 2008 Democratic presidential nomination are an African American and a woman may force America to finally face whether or not it has truly moved beyond its legacies of sexism and racism. Yet while progress has been made on both fronts, views of race and gender are remarkably different from each other. Most Americans are eager to believe that racism exists only in the past, a notion that Obama's election would help to affirm. Because Obama's personal successes are seen as a symbol of racial progress, his racial identity is a political advantage on many fronts. The country is more divided on gender, especially those roles that some see as outdated and sexist yet others remain personally invested in. At the same time, women have made substantial political progress in the past few decades, making the advancement of one woman, such as Clinton, less noteworthy than that of an African American. Thus, in contrast with Obama's emphasis on his race, Clinton tends to downplay her gender in public appearances, as it is often seen as more of a liability than an asset.

The 2006 elections were, for the technocrats and the operatives, pitting the Democratic tacticians against the Karl Rove machine. But the next election is already beginning to look quite different: 2008 may be one for the novelists.

Viewers of the election returns late on Tuesday [November 7, 2006], after all, got an early start on the iconography of the next presidential race. The cable networks' cameras cut between Sen. Hillary Rodham Clinton, thanking her supporters for an overwhelming victory in the New York Senate race, her husband standing pointedly behind, and a smiling Sen. Barack Obama of Illinois, giving cautious, professorial analysis to the television viewers. Nobody noted the significance, but it stared us all in the face: The two presumed leading contenders for the Democratic presidential nomination are a woman and an African-American.

Their candidacies—coming after elections resulting in the presumed first female speaker of the House and the second black governor since Reconstruction—suggest that the 2008 elections may play in ways that are more cultural and symbolic than tactical and political. Are Americans ready to put a black man or a woman in charge of the country? And does the hefty symbolism that Obama and Clinton would bring help one of them more than the other—in other words, is the country more racist or more sexist?

[Obama] symbolizes the possibility of a more modern America.

Democracies are awkward like this. Despite incessant polling, we really get only one moment every two years, at best, to measure how Americans feel about things, and these elections must stand as imperfect proxies for a mess of subjects: what we think about religion, whether we like being included in the international conversation, whether Northeast bluebloods would tolerate a Texan as their leader.

But when it comes to race and sex, this seems a slightly more legitimate game: The question that remains for black Americans and women isn't whether prejudice has diffused to the point that they can participate in the United States, it's whether they can legitimately hope to lead it.

Progress for Minorities and Women

Today, they may have reasons to be optimistic. Poll numbers for Clinton and Obama are among the strongest of any presidential hopefuls. It now seems nearly as common for political leaders in television shows and movies to be women or racial minorities as white men. Recent polls have found that the percentages of Americans who say they would not vote for a hypothetical black or female presidential candidate, long formidable, have dwindled into the single digits. And last Tuesday's elections put House Minority Leader Nancy Pelosi (D-Calif.) on the brink of becoming speaker and Democrat Deval Patrick, who is black, in the Massachusetts governorship.

But as the two would-be presidential candidates grapple with how to manage the legacies of their own identities, Obama seems engaged with a more problematic political feeling. Even if race is more socially crippling than gender—even if it was less likely that Obama would make it to Harvard Law than that Clinton would make it to Yale Law—the symbolism of race can also be awfully empowering to individual politicians who learn to harness it. Most Americans want to believe that the culture has moved past its racial problems, and that the symbol of that progress would be widely cheered. Compared with Clinton, says George Lakoff, a linguistics professor and Democratic message guru, "Obama clearly has it better."

Race and Gender in America

Whatever racism remains in this country, it coexists with a galloping desire to put that old race stuff behind us, to have a national Goodbye to All That moment. The most recent such occasion was Obama's much-publicized tour to promote his book of policy prescriptions, *The Audacity of Hope. The Denver Post* called him a "rock star," the *Seattle Times* found him "electrifying," and even the *Deseret News* in Salt Lake City described the "raucous greeting" he received in Utah. This rapture wasn't only because of what Obama has said; most of his audiences had not heard much from him or read much of his book. It was because he symbolizes the possibility of a more modern America.

Clinton had a best-selling autobiography and a media-heavy book tour, too, but the coverage had less to do with the symbolism she carried as a woman than with her history as Bill Clinton's wife, and with the way she was positioning herself for the future. There are many reasons for this difference, but one critical one has to do with the legacies of oppression that each inherits. While many Americans have a sincere sense of sentimentality and nostalgia for what Clinton may consider outdated gender roles, a much smaller number have that kind of feeling for racial segregation. There is the sense that, by electing a female president, the nation would be meeting a standard set by other liberal democracies; the election of a black man, by contrast, would be a particularly American achievement, an affirmation of American ideals and a celebration of American circumstances.

Obama and Race

Obama's mixed-race heritage is rarely far from his political conversation. He writes of having a Kansan mother "as white as milk," and a Kenyan father "as black as pitch." He has used his race explicitly while speaking in Africa and urging politicians there to move beyond tribalism, and implicitly while speaking in southern Illinois to punctuate an address about the challenges of globalization. In his speeches, Obama uses his simple presence as an establishment national political figure who is black to serve as a metaphorical exclamation point—a visual assurance that the country can work for everyone.

Clinton has spent a decade and a half being beaten up ... for the intersection of her gender and her politics.

This is how he used it in his most famous speech, at the 2004 Democratic National Convention: "I stand here today, grateful for the diversity of my heritage, aware that my parents' dreams live on in my two precious daughters. I stand here knowing that my story is part of the larger American story, that I owe a debt to all of those who came before me, and that, in no other country on Earth, is my story even possible."

Clinton and Gender

When Clinton gives a speech, her gender is just as evident, but she doesn't give it nearly the same kind of rhetorical prominence. She is as likely to talk about handing out buttons for Republican Barry Goldwater as a child as about what her presence as a political woman means for the country. Her most famous speech during the current political cycle dealt with a topic close to her own identity: In January 2005, she gave a widely praised talk to a group of New York state family-planning providers, telling them that the pro-choice movement had failed to acknowledge the great emotional cost involved in having an abortion. For Clinton, a hero to many women who support abortion rights, this was regarded as a particularly brave stance.

But in a speech about such a personal topic, what is most noteworthy is its impersonality. Clinton didn't mention her own experiences as a wife or a mother, but seized upon a trip she took to Romania as first lady, where she learned about the policies of the dictatorship of Nicolae Ceausescu, who tried to force every woman to have five children for the glory of the state, subjecting them to monthly roundups and reproductive exams attended by the secret police. It's a striking story, but what's even more striking is the way Clinton introduced it: "My own views of family planning and reproductive rights are heavily influenced by my travels as first lady," she said. This is not only the kind of thing that Sen. Joe Biden might say, but it also sounds suspicious: Were Clinton's views on these issues not fully formed *before* she began traveling as first lady?

Different Histories

The contrast is vivid in the two senators' autobiographies. Obama's, "Dreams From My Father," is an attempt to explain his evolving political awareness as a direct articulation of his roots. Here is the way Clinton begins her life story, "Living History": "I wasn't born a first lady or a senator. I wasn't born a Democrat. I wasn't born a lawyer or an advocate for women's rights and human rights. I wasn't born a wife or a mother."

Part of this difference is simple personal style. And there's also the matter of learned political behavior: Clinton has spent a decade and a half being beaten up, often personally and viciously, for the intersection of her gender and her politics, and it would make sense if she were trying to disconnect the two. But there is something else here.

There's a model for being post-racial, but there's no easy way to be post-gender.

The political progress of women and African-Americans has long been intertwined; the suffragette movement gained huge momentum from the complaint that black men had received the right to vote before women of any race. But when it comes to modern political leadership, women have become more present. In January [2007], the Senate will have 16 women and one African-American, while eight women and one African-American will be governors. Geraldine Ferraro was a vice presidential running mate more than 20 years ago, and still no black politician has reached that plateau.

Gender Less Noteworthy

Gender, meanwhile, may have become part of the political wallpaper. When Rep. Harold E. Ford Jr. and Maryland Lt. Gov. Michael Steele ran for [the] Senate this fall [2006], their race was mentioned in virtually every story; when Sen. Debbie Stabenow and Claire McCaskill ran, their gender was barely noted. The ferocity of national feelings about race can still be threatening; this election cycle [2006] saw the widely condemned race-baiting ads run against Ford in Tennessee. But if the nation feels its racial sins more clearly, it also has a more urgent desire to get past them. "I think gender has become more normal in leadership," said Marie Wilson, president of the White House Project, a New York nonprofit that works to develop female leaders with the goal of having a woman in the White House. "Race is a much more troubling, sadder, unresolved part of our history than the issue of gender, so it certainly looms larger."

Of course, the civil rights and women's rights movements of the 1960s have left vastly different legacies. No political figure would dare deny the saintliness of the Rev. Martin Luther King Jr.; Betty Friedan's name is a political dirty word. Repression of blacks was the stuff of massive state-leveraged cruelty—the police dogs and fire hoses—while repression of women in this country was made of quiet stuff: bras, aprons and constitutional amendments.

Post-Racial vs. Post-Gender

Obama is frequently called post-racial, the suggestion being that because he has an exotic background, Americans are looking at a newer model of a human. The metaphor works for Obama politically, because it contains the idea that his youth lets him create a more modern and inclusive brand of politics than the rhetoric of civil rights-era politicians such as Jesse Jackson. Clinton's Jesse Jacksons are Ferraro, who bombed, and Pelosi, who is still hanging around.

This is the ultimate imbalance between the would-be presidential contenders, and it's both rough on Clinton and helps explain why Obama's public presentation is so much more closely linked to his identity: There's a model for being post-racial, but there's no easy way to be post-gender.

Fredrick Harris, a political scientist at the University of Rochester, sees a post-gender future out there, and its name is Condoleezza Rice. The secretary of state, he notes, "is unmarried, has no children, is completely dedicated to her job, for pleasure she plays the piano and works and that's about it."

Clinton has made different choices, but they have their limits. Politically, she has done everything that Obama has done: She has become a serious policy professional, moved toward the center and renounced the excesses of 1960s-style identity politics. And yet these moves are received as the tacks of a smart politician. For Obama, they are received as the arrival of his race.

3

The U.S. Is More Ready for a Woman President than a Black President

Adam Nagourney

Adam Nagourney is chief political reporter for the New York Times, *where he has written about U.S. politics since 1996.*

Both women and African Americans have made substantial political gains, but as a group, women have clearly made more progress than blacks when it comes to elected office. For instance, in 2007, nine states have women governors while only one has a black governor. On the other hand, African American Barack Obama, one of the leading Democratic contenders for the 2008 presidential election, is unique among black politicians, which accounts for the optimism many feel about his chances for election. Still, most black voters, including Obama himself, are skeptical about America's willingness to elect a black president.

After a 217-year march of major presidential nominees who were, without exception, white and male, the 2008 campaign may offer voters a novel choice.

But as Barack Obama, the senator from Illinois whose father is from Kenya, spends this weekend exploring a presidential bid in New Hampshire, and Hillary Rodham Clinton, the first woman to represent New York in the Senate, calls potential supporters in Iowa, the question remains: Are Americans prepared to elect an African-American or a woman as president?

Or, to look at it from the view of Democrats hungry for victory in 2008, is the nation more likely to vote for a woman or an African-American for president?

Without question, women and blacks have made significant progress in winning office. The new [2007] Congress will include 71 women—one of whom will be the first female speaker of the House—compared with 25 when Representative Geraldine Ferraro, a Queens Democrat, became the first woman to run as a major-party vice presidential candidate in 1984. There will be 43 blacks in the new Congress, compared with 13 when the Congressional Black Caucus was formed in 1969. A Gallup Poll in September [2006] showed a steady rise in the number of people who expect the nation to elect a woman or an African-American as president one day: Americans, it seems, are much more open to these choices than, say, someone who is an atheist or who is gay.

Times are indeed changing. But how much?

Over the past eight years, in the view of analysts from both parties, the country has shifted markedly on the issue of gender, to the point where they say voters could very well be open to electing a woman in 2008. That is reflected, they say, in polling data and in the continued success of women running for office, in red and blue states alike. "The country is ready," said Senator Elizabeth Dole, the North Carolina Republican, who ran unsuccessfully for president in 2000. "I'm not saying it's going to happen in '08. But the country is ready."

There will be one black governor next year ... By contrast, women will be governors of nine states.

A Black President?

By contrast, for all the excitement stirred by Mr. Obama, it is much less certain that an African-American could win a presidential election. Not as many blacks have been elected to prominent positions as women. Some high-profile black candidates—Harold Ford Jr., a Democrat running for the Senate in Tennessee, and Michael Steele, a Republican Senate candidate in Maryland—lost in November [2006]. And demographics might be an obstacle as well: Black Americans are concentrated in about 25 states—typically blue ones, like New York and California. While black candidates cannot assume automatic support from black voters, they would at least provide a base. In states without big black populations, the candidate's crossover appeal must be huge.

"All evidence is that a white female has an advantage over a black male—for reasons of our cultural heritage," said the Rev. Jesse L. Jackson, the civil rights leader who ran for president in 1984 and 1988. Still, he said, for African-American and female candidates, "It's easier—emphatically so."

Ms. Ferraro offered a similar sentiment. "I think it's more realistic for a woman than it is for an African-American," said Ms. Ferraro. "There is a certain amount of racism that exists in the United States—whether it's conscious or not it's true."

"Women are 51 percent of the population," she added.

Many analysts suggested that changing voter attitudes can best be measured in choices for governors, since they, like presidents, are judged as chief executives, rather than legislators. There will be one black governor next year [2007]—Deval L. Patrick in Massachusetts, the second in the nation since Reconstruction.

By contrast, women will be governors of nine states, including Washington, Arizona and Michigan, all potential battleground states in 2008, a fact that is no doubt viewed favorably by advisers to Mrs. Clinton.

"Voters are getting more comfortable with seeing governors as C.E.O.'s of states," said Gov. Kathleen Sebelius, a Kansas Democrat. Gov. Jennifer M. Granholm, a Michigan Democrat who won a second term last month [November 2006], said in an interview that when she first ran, she had to work harder. "Not this time," she said in an interview. "They are used to a woman being governor."

Obama's Appeal

Of course, governors don't have to handle national security. And Mrs. Clinton has used her six years in the Senate to try to counter the stereotype that women would not be as strong on the issue, especially with the nation at war. Mrs. Clinton won a seat on the Armed Services Committee, and was an early supporter of the war in Iraq.

Mr. Obama is in many ways an unusual African-American politician, and that is why many Democrats, and Republicans, view him as so viable.

Mr. Obama is a member of a post-civil-rights generation of black politicians and is not identified with leaders like Mr. Jackson and the Rev. Al Sharpton of New York, who are polarizing to many white voters. He has a warm and commanding campaign presence that, as he showed in Illinois, cut across color lines.

Mr. Obama said that many black voters he spoke with have serious questions about whether America is ready to elect an African American president.

Donna Brazile, a prominent Democratic strategist who is black, said that she had been deluged with e-mail messages from people looking to volunteer for Mr. Obama—and that most of the requests were from white voters.

Moreover, there is abundant evidence that attitudes toward black candidates are changing among white voters. In Tennessee, Mr. Ford lost his bid to become the state's first black senator since Reconstruction, but by only three percentage points.

Surveys of voters leaving the polls showed that 40 percent of white voters supported Mr. Ford, compared with 95 percent of black voters. More intriguing, the final result was the same as what the exit polls had suggested. Before this, in many races involving black candidates, the polls predicted that they would do better than they actually did—presumably because voters were reluctant to tell questioners they did not support the African-American.

That said, Mr. Ford lost his race after Republicans aired an advertisement that Democrats said was explicitly racist. Many Democrats said a lesson of the loss was that racial appeals still have force, particularly in the South.

Other Factors

Race and gender are big issues in American politics, but they are not the only ones, particularly in the coming race. Mr. Obama, should he run, may find his lack of experience will be far more troublesome to voters than his color. He is 45 and serving his first term as senator.

Mr. Obama said that many black voters he spoke with have serious questions about whether America is ready to elect an African-American president.

"I think there is a protectiveness and a skepticism within the African-American community that is grounded in their experiences," Mr. Obama said in an interview. "But the skepticism doesn't mean there's a lack of support."

David A. Bositis, senior political analyst with the Joint Center for Political and Economic Studies, a nonpartisan Washington group that studies black issues, said that it would certainly be hard, but not impossible for an African-American candidate to win.

"I certainly felt in the '90s that if Colin Powell had been nominated on a major party ticket, he would have had a very good chance to win," Mr. Bositis said. "If it's the right black candidate, I do think there is propensity to elect a black. But it has to be the right black candidate."

4

The U.S. Is Ready for a Black President

Mike Bruton

Mike Bruton is the editor of the Sunday Philadelphia Tribune.

The popularity of 2008 presidential candidate Senator Barack Obama has prompted the question of whether America is ready for a black president. Results of the 2006 midterm election provide indisputable evidence that American politics have come a long way. Some of this recent progress may be attributed to a new generation of minority candidates, as well as changing voting patterns. Still, there remains a faction of American voters who will not vote for a candidate if he or she is black. This residual racism was especially evident during recent campaign ads run by Bob Corker against his black opponent, Harold Ford Jr. Yet the national media's critical reaction to these ads further illustrates America's growing intolerance of racism in the political arena.

While Sen. Barack Obama tours the country, leaving in his wake throng after throng of adoring supporters, a question hangs over his head like the most pregnant of pauses.

Is America ready for a Black president?

It is a query worthy of careful handling, one that is always thorny, never comfortable, but has been made irrepressible by not only Obama-mania but by several factors that have emerged in biracial electoral politics in the 21st century.

Mike Bruton, "The Door Inches Open for a Black President," *Philadelphia Tribune*, vol. 4, no. 14, Feb. 18, 2007, pp. 1A–2A. Copyright © 2007 Philadelphia Tribune. Reproduced by permission.

The Pew Research Center [in February 2007] released the results of a study that suggests Americans might be ready to elect a Black person to the highest office in the land.

The poll also tears away the long-held premise that 10 percentage points should always be subtracted from the number that an African-American candidate receives in a statewide or nationwide tracking poll because white voters, embarrassed about their racial bias, lie to pollsters.

"African-Americans are now able to come through old barriers," top Democratic strategist Donna Brazile told *USA Today* just days before the midterm election last November [2006]: "Whether they make it to the finish line is another thing, but the door has been left ajar."

Judging by what happened at the polls on Election Day, major Black candidates did indeed get through that door.

Many attribute that to demographic and generational changes in the candidates themselves. Unlike senior Black candidates, the younger breed is too young to have been involved in the civil rights movement and haven't gone to historically Black colleges.

In 2003, 92 percent of Americans said they would vote for a Black candidate while only 6 percent said they would not.

This younger group, which includes Obama, [Deval] Patrick—who recently became Massachusetts's first Black governor, former Congressman Harold Ford—who narrowly (51–48 percent) lost a Tennessee Senate bid, and Keith Ellison, who in November became the first Muslim elected to the U.S. House of Representatives, often favor pragmatism over emotion, and many are from Ivy League colleges or powerful law firms.

"I don't even see him as Black," said a 54-year-old white Massachusetts voter of Patrick prior to the election. Injecting humor, the man added, "It looks to me that he has a deep tan."

Changes in Voting Behavior

White voters, some believe, are beginning to function more like their Black, Asian, and Latino counterparts, who have always voted for white candidates, even when they were running against a candidate of their race, if that white candidate agreed with them on issues and had proven he or she could be trusted.

Chicago's Madeline Haithcock, a Black woman seeking re-election in a very competitive aldermanic race in a majority Black ward, summed the scenario up.

"There is nothing racial about this," Haithcock told the *Chicago Sun-Times*. "When are we going to get over that?"

Haithcock is the incumbent running in the South Loop and Westside Second Ward contest, which includes two white candidates.

"You know, I'm 63 years old," she continued. "I think I'm tired of fighting that battle. I want to get along, and I know in my ward I don't go say, 'Oh I'm not going to do this for this white person, but I'm going to do it for the Black person or the Hispanic.' That doesn't make sense."

In a *Newsweek* poll conducted last year [2006], only three percent of respondents said they would not vote for a qualified Black candidate for president. You don't have to go too far back in the past to find a much higher level of intolerance for African-American presidential aspirations.

Gallup has asked this question since 1958 and most recently, in 2003, 92 percent of Americans said they would vote for a Black candidate while only six percent said they would not.

In the first Gallup poll posing this question, in 1958, 53 percent said they would not vote for a Black candidate, and as recently as 1984, 16 percent said they wouldn't.

Obama's Chances

In January [2007] polls conducted by *Newsweek* and ABC/ Washington Post, Obama was slightly ahead of Sen. John McCain, R-Ariz., one of the top Republican presidential candidates, while Sen. Hillary Clinton, D-N.Y., the Democratic frontrunner, did slightly better against McCain.

Obama led McCain 48–42 percent in the *Newsweek* poll and 47–45 in the ABC/Washington Post poll, with Clinton leading 50–44 and 50–45.

The undecided column showed the difference, as Obama had 10 percent unsure in one and seven percent in the other.

That could change, for better or worse, as Obama gets more exposure.

So far, exposure has helped the former Illinois state representative from Chicago.

The national media hammered the [Bob] Corker camp, perhaps proving American journalism is also ready for a black president.

"I knew from the day he walked into this chamber that he was destined for great things," Kirk Dillard, a leading Illinois state senator and a white Republican, told *The New Yorker*. "In Republican circles, we've always feared that Barack would become a rock star of American politics. He's to me left of me on gun control, abortion, but he can really work with Republicans."

Undoubtedly, progress has been made and, if political advances of Black candidates form the measuring stick, Americans have grown more tolerant since the 1980s and 1990s, when there was still a sizeable block of the electorate that wouldn't vote for African-Americans.

Yet the shadow of racism and intolerance is still a factor for both Black and white voters.

"There remains a non-trivial faction of white voters who will not vote for a candidate simply because (the candidate) is Black," Vincent Hutchings, a University of Michigan political scientist, told *USA Today*. "We are kidding ourselves if we argue these people have disappeared from the landscape."

Residual Racism

The fact that questionable ads, specifically in the Massachusetts gubernatorial election and the Tennessee senatorial election, were brazenly used last November [2006] serves notice that cynicism and discrimination are still with us.

Patrick's opponent, Kerry Healey, ran a TV spot showing a white woman being stalked as she walks in a parking garage as the announcer says, "He (Patrick) should be ashamed—not governor."

Healey said because Patrick had advocated the parole of a rapist, the ad was fair. Patrick disagreed.

"There were a lot of reasons why people equated those ads with the Willie Horton ad," Patrick said, referring to the infamous spot the George H.W. Bush campaign used against Michael Dukakis in the 1988 presidential race.

The ad Bob Corker's campaign used against Harold Ford suggested the Congressman was a big partygoer and ended with a white woman suggestively urging Ford, to "call me."

In this instance, the national media hammered the Corker camp, perhaps proving American journalism is also ready for a Black president.

Many national pundits and newsmen pointed out that right after the "call me" followed the slogan that Ford was "Just not Right"—which was uncomfortably close to "Just not White."

The *Columbia Journalism Review* commented, "That's how the press begins to show that it's ready for a Black president, and slowly, so does America."

5

The U.S. Is Not Ready for a Black President

Ron Mwangaguhunga

Ron Mwangaguhunga is a writer living in Brooklyn, New York. He is former editor of MacDirectory.

The only black U.S. presidents that Americans have experienced are portrayed in TV comedies and science fiction movies. In reality, it is clear that the U.S. is still not ready for a black president since there is still not a black member of the Senate. John F. Kennedy made history when he was elected the first Roman Catholic president in 1960, but religious belief and racial identity are two different things. Although many people jest that Bill Clinton was America's first black president, in truth his loyalties to black Americans faltered more than once. Unfortunately, the time when the United States will have a president who is actually black appears to be in the not-so-near future.

Despite his stately demeanor, his unquestioned grasp of the minutiae of public policy and his formidable presence, Chris Rock is not the first "black president;" he just played one in a mini-hit this past March [2003].

"Head of State" is the most recent in a fashionable series of fictional portrayals of what life might be like if only blacks headed the U.S. government. Chris Tucker's New Line project tentatively titled "Guess Who's President"—a comedy, of course—will have footage of Bill Clinton, Nelson Mandela

Ron Mwangaguhunga, "When Will We Have an Authentic Black President?" *The Mississippi Link*, vol. 11, no. 30, Jul. 30, 2003, p. A4. Copyright © 2003 Mississippi Link. Reproduced by permission.

and Bahrain's crown prince endorsing Tucker's fictional bid. The idea of a black president might transcend the genre of comedy if only we could elect and keep a black seat in the Senate.

But Bill Clinton notwithstanding [in 1998, novelist Toni Morrison referred to Bill Clinton as America's "first black President"], America has never come close to electing a black president. The entertainment world, however, is bewitched by this possibility. Up until now, the idea of a black president has most often been portrayed at the safe, ironic distance of comedy, as in the case of "Head of State," or, less frequently, in the science fiction genre (how telling is that?), with Morgan Freeman in "Deep Impact," or Zeus "Tiny" Lister, Jr. in Luc Besson's "The Fifth Element" serving as prime examples.

In genres of fiction, the idea of a black president is widely portrayed; it is in reality, alas, that the issue eludes us.

There is, of course, the Colin Powell factor. Everyone says that they would love Colin Powell to run for the presidency ("Run Colin, Run"), but in reality would he actually stand a chance? Possibly, but as he has never been elected to office, the question is a toss-up.

Being a Roman Catholic, which is volitional, and being black, which is congenital, are not the same kettle of fish.

Could Colin Powell go in and sweep the Southern primaries on Super Tuesday as a Republican candidate needs to? Can you imagine the Secretary of State, hand held high, at the state capital of South Carolina, where there is still furor in the air over the Confederate flag issue? [In 2000, both state houses of South Carolina voted to remove the Confederate flag from the dome of the statehouse, where it had flown since 1962.] No, me neither.

The White Male Presidency

In the history of the U.S. there has never been anything but a constant succession of white male presidents. Oddly, little has been said about this embarrassing subject. As I see it, America probably has to break a few more social barriers before a black president could be elected.

To be frank: We are not ready to have a black man or, for that matter, a black woman as president. I regard here the Senate as the Great Cultural Barometer as to how far the U.S. has evolved with regards to allowing minorities access to its vital institutions of power.

One could almost make a parlor game of guessing whether or not a black, Latino or a woman could be elected in our lifetime. But I'd rather not, though, for the reason that such a game might become depressing for the black realist.

The effervescent John F. Kennedy was the first elected Roman Catholic President of the U.S. in 1960. The election of an Irish-American Roman Catholic in Anglo-Saxon Protestant America was a small but significant victory that broke unspoken social barriers. Kennedy's religiosity was, to be sure, an issue during the [1960] Nixon race, and he charismatically got in front of the issue and effectively neutralized it. But being a Roman Catholic, which is volitional, and being black, which is congenital, are not the same kettle of fish.

The only optimistic message I can give out is that [the first black president] will be before the first black pope.

[In July 2003] Latinos were officially recognized as the largest minority, extrapolated from recent census figures. Asians and blacks have precisely one governor in American history each. And [in 2003] there are currently no blacks or Asians in the U.S. Senate.

A Truly Black President

At the outset, it seemed that black elites embraced the idea of Bill Clinton as black. One remembers Chris Tucker—as well as the rest of the room—star-struck at President Clinton at the 32nd National Association for the Advancement of Colored People Image Awards.

But Bill Clinton is not black, at least not to the politically sophisticated. Clinton publicly criticized Sista Souljah [a Hip Hop artist and activist quoted by the *Washington Post* in 1992 as saying in response to the Los Angeles riots that "if black people kill black people everyday, why not have a week and kill white people?"] at a Rainbow Coalition event, in front of a stunned Jesse Jackson, to win over white moderates; Clinton was showing the Bubba vote that he knows how to punish those blacks who will not behave. The maneuver made him a serious player in the dark and conservative backrooms of the Southern primaries. No self-respecting black man would have done that in public for moderate white votes; nor would any self-respecting black man slap Haiti's Jean-Bertrand Aristide into compliance in quite the manner that Bill Clinton did. No, Virginia, Bill Clinton is not black, but his heart sure is, on occasion.

But when will we actually have an authentic black President? I would like to say here that we will have a black president within the century. The only optimistic message I can give out is that it will be before the first black Pope which, in my reasoning, appears to be several centuries away. Then again, the Catholic Church has only recently accepted Galileo's interpretation of reality, so the question of centuries may be overly optimistic.

6

The U.S. Is Ready for a Black President Not Descended from African Slaves

Debra J. Dickerson

Debra Dickerson is a writer whose work has appeared in the New Republic, *the* Washington Post, Slate, *and* Essence. *She has published two books, including* The End of Blackness, *which examines the evolution of blackness in America.*

Illinois Senator Barack Obama has attracted enormous attention since he announced his 2008 presidential candidacy. Surprisingly, reactions from black leaders like Jesse Jackson and Al Sharpton have been lukewarm, in part because they are not certain which direction Obama's loyalties would lean were he elected. Because Obama's mother was a white American and his father was Kenyan, he is not actually "black" in the the usual American sense of the word. As a result, he represents to white Americans a non-threatening means to assuage their guilt.

I am confident that I have held out longer than any other pundit to weigh in on both the phenomenon that is Barack Obama and the question of whether race will trump gender as America looks toward election 2008.

I had irritably avoided columnizing on these crucial topics (though I have been quoted by others) for several, somewhat unorthodox, reasons. First, because the [Senator Hillary]

Clinton-Obama stand-off has been more than well-covered—and in an overly simplistic, insubstantial, annoyingly celebritized way. . . .

I had also held off from writing about Obama because the tsunami of attention and adulation this son of a Kenyan goat herder has had to navigate is just too much, too soon. . . .

Those in the civil rights machine are putting the brakes on Obama-mania and feigning objectivity when it comes to his candidacy. . . .

Without a doubt, the Reverends [Jesse] Jackson and [Al] Sharpton's main reason for giving him the faux high hat is a determination to potty-train the upstart, flex their own muscles, and ensure that there will remain a place for them at the power broker's table. Perhaps most important, they're no doubt waiting for his reverse Sister Souljah moment.[1] Just as the Negro-friendly Bill Clinton had to gamble on retaining that base while reassuring whites that he knew how to keep blacks in line, so Obama has to reassure blacks he is unafraid to tell whites things that whites decidedly do not want to hear. Never having been "black for a living" with protest politics or any form of racial oppositionality, he'll need to assure the black powers that be that he won't dis the politics of blackness (and, hence, them), however much he might keep it on mute. He didn't attain power through traditional black channels (not a minister, no time at the NAACP [National Association for the Advancement of Colored People]) so, technically, he owes the civil rights lobby nothing, but they need him in their debt. Homie has some rings to kiss and a kente-cloth [a fabric native to Ghana, a worldwide symbol of African heritage] pocket square to buy. Still, the overtures he needs to make are purely symbolic; he's irresistible, and the black bourgeoisie won't be able to keep their hands off him. For all his bluster,

---

1. In 1992, Hip-hop artist and activist Sister Souljah was quoted in the *Washington Post* as saying in response to the Los Angeles riots, "If black people kill black people everyday, why not have a week and kill white people?"

even Jackson recently admitted to CNN that "all of my heart leans toward Barack." The black embrace is Obama's to lose.

"Black," in our political and social reality, means those descended from West African slaves.

Also, and more subtly, when the handsome Obama doesn't look eastern (versus western) African, he looks like his white mother; not so subliminally, that's partially why whites can embrace him but blacks fear that one day he'll go Tiger Woods on us and get all race transcendent [Woods, who is of African, Asian, Native American, and European descent, refers to himself as "Caublinasian"] (he might well have never been in the running without a traditionally black spouse and kids). Notwithstanding their silence on the subject, blacks at the top are aware (and possibly troubled?) by Obama's lottery winnings: "black" but not black. Not descended from West African slaves brought to America, he steps into the benefits of black progress (like Harvard Law School) without having borne any of the burden, and he gives the white folks plausible deniability of their unwillingness to embrace blacks in public life. None of Obama's doing, of course, but nonetheless a niggling sort of freebie for which he'll have to do some groveling.

Which brings me to the main reason I delayed writing about Obama. For me, it was a trick question in a game I refused to play. Since the issue was always framed as a battle between gender and race (read: non-whiteness—the question is moot when all the players are white), I didn't have the heart (or the stomach) to point out the obvious: Obama isn't black.

"Black" in America

"Black," in our political and social reality, means those descended from West African slaves. Voluntary immigrants of African descent (even those descended from West Indian slaves) are just that, voluntary immigrants of African descent with markedly different outlooks on the role of race in their lives and in politics. At a minimum, it can't be assumed that a Nigerian cabdriver and a third-generation Harlemite have more in common than the fact a cop won't bother to make the distinction. They're both "black" as a matter of skin color and DNA, but only the Harlemite, for better or worse, is politically and culturally black, as we use the term.

We know a great deal about black people. We know next to nothing about immigrants of African descent (woe be unto blacks when the latter groups find their voice and start saying all kinds of things we don't want said). That rank-and-file black voters might not bother to make this distinction as long as Obama acts black and does us proud makes them no less complicit in this shell game we're playing because everybody wins. (For all the hoopla over Obama, though, most blacks still support Sen. Clinton, with her long relationships in the community and the spillover from President Clinton's wide popularity.)

Since [Obama] had no part in our racial history, he is free of it.

Whites, on the other hand, are engaged in a paroxysm of self-congratulation; he's the equivalent of Stephen Colbert's "black friend." Swooning over nice, safe Obama means you aren't a racist. I honestly can't look without feeling pity, and indeed mercy, at whites' need for absolution. For all our sakes, it seemed (again) best not to point out the obvious: You're not embracing a black man, a descendant of slaves. You're *replacing* the black man with an immigrant of recent African descent of whom you can approve without feeling either guilty or frightened. If he were Ronald Washington from Detroit, even with the same résumé, he wouldn't be getting this kind of love. Washington would have to earn it, not just show promise of it, and even then whites would remain wary.

I'll go so far as to say that a white woman will be the Democratic nominee for president before a black descendant of American slaves. Even if Obama invokes slavery and Jim Crow [Jim Crow laws were state and local laws in place in some U.S states between 1876 and 1965 that enforced racial segregation], he does so as one who stands outside, one who emotes but still merely informs. One who can be respectfully tolerated because there's a limit to how far he can go in invoking history. He signals to whites that the racial turmoil and stalemate of the last generation are past and that with him comes a new day in politics when whites needn't hold back for fear of being thought racist.

To say that Obama isn't black is merely to say that, by virtue of his white American mom and his Kenyan dad who abandoned both him and America, he is an American of African immigrant extraction. It is also to point out the continuing significance of the slave experience to the white American psyche; it's not we who can't get over it. It's you. Lumping us all together (which blacks also do from sloppiness and ignorance, and as a way to dominate the race issue and to force immigrants of African descent to subordinate their preferences to ours) erases the significance of slavery and continuing racism while giving the appearance of progress. Though actually, it *is* a kind of progress. And that's why I break my silence: Obama, with his non-black ass, is doing us all a favor.

Since he had no part in our racial history, he is free of it. And once he's opened the door to even an awkward embrace of candidates of color for the highest offices, the door will stay open. A side door, but an open door. Yet until Obama survives the scourging he's about to receive from Hillary Clinton (God help him if he really did lie about his Muslim background [Although Obama is a Christian, he attended a Muslim School as a child, which has ignited some controversy]) and the electoral process, no candidate of color will ever be taken seriously. Clinton isn't about to leave the stage in the name of racial progress, and the pundit class has only just begun to take apart the senator's record, associates and bank accounts. Still, this *is* progress. A non-black on the down low about his non-blackness is about to get what blacks have always asked for: to be judged on his merits. So let's all just pretend that we've really overcome.

7

The U.S. Is Ready for a Woman President

Bob Barr

Bob Barr represented Georgia in the U.S. House of Representatives from 1995 to 2003. He currently practices law and occupies the 21st Century Liberties Chair for Freedom and Privacy at the American Conservative Union.

Since November 2005, several countries in Africa, South America, and Europe have elected women as their leaders for the first time. All of these women have impressive political records, and some have personal histories that might have kept them out of office in the past. These elections signal a shift in the global consciousness that should pave the way for the U.S. to elect its first female leader in the near future as well.

Winds of change are sweeping the globe, and they have nothing to do with Iraq, Afghanistan, terrorism, or even George W. Bush.

Citizens in countries from Western Europe to Africa to South America are electing women leaders in regions that have rarely—if ever—taken such steps in the past. Whether those winds reach the shores of the world's last superpower standing remains to be seen. But leaves are already rustling on the banks of both the Potomac and the Hudson rivers. Two political figures of national prominence—U.S. Sen. Hillary Rodham Clinton (D-N.Y.) and Secretary of State Condoleezza Rice—have their sails ready to catch that wind if it arrives.

Bob Barr, "U.S. Might Be Next to Elect a Female Leader," *The Atlanta Journal Constitution*, Jan. 25, 2006, p. A15. Reproduced by permission of the author.

It has been more than a quarter of a century since Margaret Thatcher—"The Iron Lady"—stunned the Western world by being elected to the prime ministership of our closest ally [the United Kingdom, in 1979]. That was a novelty to many Americans and was not seen as posing a true threat to the male dominance that has maintained a monopoly on the U.S. presidency since George Washington took our nation's first oath of office in the late 18th century. Many Americans remained vaguely aware that women had served as prime ministers in a number of other faraway lands with exotic names—Sri Lanka, India, Pakistan and Israel, among other countries whose names most Americans could not even pronounce. However, the notion that a member of the "fairer sex" could in fact rise to occupy the most powerful political post on the planet remained more a thing of Hollywood's imagination than of serious political analysis.

Bachelet's election is particularly illustrative of the deep and wide changes that are sweeping our planet's political landscape.

Events of the past three months, however, have cast this debate—if indeed it even remains such—in an entirely different light. Reflect for a moment on what has happened on the world stage just since November [2005]:

- Africa—a continent that has never elected a woman chief executive—has seen its first woman [Ellen Johnson-Sirleaf] sworn in as a nation's chief executive, in Liberia. The transition from male rule to the new era was accomplished without bloodshed or upheaval on a continent hardly known for such transitions. The inaugural ceremony was given the imprimatur of the United States by having first lady Laura Bush attend.

- Germany, which has given the Western world some of its most iron-fisted male rulers—from Otto von Bismarck to the fiendish Adolf Hitler—has for the very first time elected a woman to serve as chancellor, Angela Merkel.

- In South America, the continent where the term "macho" was coined and still serves as the bedrock for much of its countries' social culture, Chile has just elected its first female president, Michelle Bachelet.

The achievements of none of these new leaders can be attributed to factors divorced from their skills and political acumen. Each had to fight long and hard to reach the point at which they would be taken seriously as a possible contender for the top job. Two—Bachelet of Chile and Liberia's Ellen Johnson-Sirleaf—served time in prison for political crimes. All three served with distinction in top posts in their governments prior to running for the top job.

The time for change had come, not as a shock or aberration, but as a smooth and logical step.

A Global Trend

Bachelet's election is particularly illustrative of the deep and wide changes that are sweeping our planet's political landscape. Virtually every taboo that in decades past would have argued against this 54-year-old woman being elected president was broken in the course of her ascension. She is an opponent of the current regime and was imprisoned and exiled by its earlier occupants; and she is a dedicated socialist in a country that has, since the 1973 coup that ousted the Marxist Salvador Allende, served as a tribute to free-market economics. In a continent with the strongest ties to the Catholic Church outside of the Vatican, not only is she a single mom, but she does not shy away from the fact that one of her children was born out of wedlock.

By every historical measure, none of these women should now be serving (or about to serve) as heads of state. Does this represent a true global trend or simply reflect a handful of isolated examples in which unusual national factors produce aberrations? I suspect that the future lies in the former description, not the latter.

The elections of both Merkel and Bachelet were preceded by periods in which the party in power had run the course of a lengthy stay at the helm. Malaise, if not unrest, was setting in, as was drift and fatigue with the governing crowd (sound familiar?). The culture of both countries and regions had already shifted in many respects from the post–World War II and subsequent Cold War mentality of the tough male as the very definition of the modern leader. Women had clearly proved their mettle in Cabinet posts; the daily news was being presented 24/7 on cable news networks overwhelmingly dominated by female broadcasters. The time for change had come, not as a shock or aberration, but as a smooth and logical step.

While that culture change in other continents does not automatically translate into a gender change at 1600 Pennsylvania Ave., the seeds are not only sown but thriving. Whether Hillary Clinton or Condoleezza Rice, or another woman candidate, will reap the crop that has been thus sown remains to be seen; but the planet will no longer be knocked off its axis if she does.

8

The U.S. Is Not Ready for a Woman President

Carole Kennedy

Carole Kennedy is an associate professor of political science at San Diego State University. Her work focuses on campaigns, elections, and women in politics and has been published in Po-litical Research Quarterly, American Journal of Political Science, and White House Studies.

For years, many social commentators have claimed that the U.S. was ready for a woman president, citing polls that showed a large percentage of Americans saying they would vote for a quali-fied female candidate. However, the problematic nature of such polls has not been taken into account, especially those polls that pose such a controversial question to the public. The significance of the number of Americans who say they would not *be willing to vote for a woman has also been downplayed. There is consid-erable evidence that the public has different expectations for fe-male candidates than for male candidates, resulting in a percep-tion that women are less suited for the nation's highest political office than men. These disadvantages can be readily seen in the unsuccessful campaign of Elizabeth Dole, presidential candidate in 2000.*

Roughly twenty women have declared themselves candi-dates for the U.S. presidency throughout its history. The first was Victoria Woodhull, who ran in 1872. Other notable

Carole Kennedy, "Is the United States Ready for a Woman President? Is the Pope Prot-estant?" *Anticipating Madam President*, Eds. Robert P. Watson and Ann Gordon, Boul-der, CO: Lynne Rienner Publishers, Inc., 2003, pp. 131–43. Copyright © 2002 by Lynne Rienner Publishers, Inc. All rights reerved. Reproduced by permission.

candidates include Senator Margaret Chase Smith (R-1964) and Representative Shirley Chisholm (D-1972). In 1984, Geraldine Ferraro [runningmate of fellow Democrat Walter Mondale] became the first and only woman vice presidential candidate on a major party ticket. Elizabeth Dole's tepid attempt to capture the Republican Party nomination for president in 1999 reintroduced the question to a whole new generation of Americans and inspired debate regarding the readiness of the American public to finally seriously consider a woman president.

Supporters of the notion that the United States was really ready this time pointed to public opinion polls that showed a remarkable 92 percent of Americans indicated that they would be willing to vote for a qualified woman for the highest office in the land. What tended to be downplayed in most of these popular analyses was the truly mixed picture that public opinion polling reveals about American attitudes toward women in general and the viability of a woman candidate for the presidency in particular. In addition, although Dole faced criticism that she had no prior elective experience, there was scant attention paid to the dearth of women in other executive positions of power in the United States. A total of nineteen women have served as governors of states, and as of 2002 there were currently five elected women state executives. There are more women in the U.S. Senate now than there have ever been, and yet women represented a mere 13 percent of that august body in 2002. Finally, almost all popular analyses of U.S. readiness to elect a woman president neglect to take into account scholarly research that has identified more subtle attitudinal barriers to a woman president, as well as persistent structural features of American society that hamper the possibilities for women to assume real political power. . . .

Public Opinion Polls

Many popular and scholarly works on the topic suggest that public opinion polling reveals a steady climb in the number of

Americans willing to vote for a woman for president. As far back as 1937, the Gallup poll repeatedly asked Americans the following question: "If your party nominated a woman for president, would you vote for her if she were qualified for the job?" Whereas only 33 percent of respondents in 1937 answered in the affirmative, that proportion has increased fairly steadily over the years. The most recent Gallup poll that included this question (1999) reveals that fully 92 percent of Americans are willing to vote for a qualified woman for president. Let us take this statistic at its face value and consider its implications.

There is a discrepancy in results, depending upon how the question regarding voting for a woman president is phrased.

Seven percent of Americans polled in 1999 have indicated that they would not vote for a qualified woman for president (1 percent report having no opinion). Losing 7 percent of the presidential vote presents something of a problem for an otherwise qualified presidential candidate. Historically, the popular vote in presidential elections has varied among the two major party candidates from a very large difference of 24 percent in the 1972 election to the infinitesimal 0.2 percent in the 1960 and 1976 elections. If any given woman candidate starts out with a seven-point deficit in the popular vote, she will be hard-pressed to overcome that deficit in a close presidential election. That is especially important in the coming decade because the electorate is very closely split along partisan and ideological lines. Although critics will no doubt find this assessment pessimistic—seeing the glass as 7 percent empty instead of 92 percent full—the fact that six out of the past thirteen presidential elections were decided by a margin below 7 percent suggests that the figure is far from insignificant.

The Gallup poll question is but one of several attempts by pollsters and political scientists to effectively measure the amount of discrimination likely to be encountered when a woman candidate actually confronts the U.S. electorate. Other polls paint a much gloomier picture. In a February 23, 2001, press release, the White House Project—a nonprofit, nonpartisan organization dedicated to electing a woman president by 2008—reported the findings from its Internet poll, in which 26,000 women and 20,000 men responded to a question assessing their likelihood of voting for a female president. Fifty-nine percent of respondents indicated that they were very willing to vote for a woman president, another 26 percent indicated that they were somewhat willing to vote for a woman president, and 15 percent of respondents stated that they would not be willing to vote for a woman. Within the same press release, the president of the White House Project, Marie C. Wilson, stated: "The message of our survey is clear: Americans, regardless of their party or gender, are ready and willing to vote for a woman president." This analysis of the poll results [is] not surprising, given the agenda of the pollsters. However, a fifteen-point deficit would have cost a woman candidate the presidency in nine out of the past thirteen presidential elections.

Discrepancies Among Poll Results

Survey evidence is also mixed depending upon the question wording. A survey of several such assessments of public opinion over the past twenty-five years reveals an even greater concern. Although most Americans report that they personally would be willing to vote for a woman president, other polls show that a majority of Americans still believe that the country is not ready to elect a woman president. I refer to this phenomenon as the "third person effect." This discrepancy also points out the difficulty of accurately gauging public opinion on issues in which there is a "socially desirable response" that might lead individuals to provide the socially acceptable response rather than their true predilections. An illustrative example of how the socially desirable response phenomenon can affect elections was revealed in the 1982 California gubernatorial race. Exit polls suggested that Democratic candidate Tom Bradley (an African-American) had beaten his Republican opponent, George Deukmejian. Yet when the ballots were finally counted, Deukmejian emerged victorious by a slim margin of 53,515 votes, out of nearly 7.5 million votes cast. A Field poll conducted on election day found that 4 percent of those polled indicated they had supported Deukmejian because they did not wish to vote for a black person. Scholarly assessments of the 1982 election disagree as to whether racial prejudice played a decisive role in the outcome. However, the discrepancy between exit polls conducted on the day of the election and the final outcome suggest that many who reported having voted for Tom Bradley did not.

There is a discrepancy in results, depending upon how the question regarding voting for a woman president is phrased. The traditional Gallup poll measure has shown an increasing number of respondents over time who indicate that they would be willing to vote for a qualified woman of their party for president. Although 73 percent of respondents said they would be willing to do so in 1975, fully 92 percent responded in the affirmative in 1999. However, a side-by-side comparison of these responses to differently worded questions on the same subject illustrates the third-person effect. In 1984, for example, while the Gallup poll showed that 78 percent of respondents indicated that they would vote for a woman for president, an NBC News Poll conducted by Harris and Associates found that only 17 percent of respondents believed that the voters of this country were ready to elect a woman president. A similar discrepancy was evident in 1999, when the Gallup poll showed that 92 percent of respondents would vote for a woman for president, whereas a CBS News Poll conducted by Harris and Associates found that only 48 percent of respondents believed that the United States was ready to elect a woman president.

Several scholarly studies have suggested that gender stereotyping of female candidates for political office is prevalent and can impede their success.

A comparison of the Gallup poll question to the General Social Survey (GSS), another barometer of political attitudes toward women in politics that has been included in annual Gallup polls over time reveals that the only direct comparison by year occurred in 1975, when 23 percent of respondents to the Gallup poll said that they were not willing to vote for a woman for president, and 35 percent of respondents to the GSS poll indicated that "women should take care of running their homes and leave running the country up to men." Although a direct comparison in the 1990s is not possible, the 1996 GSS survey showed 16 percent of respondents agreeing that women should take care of running their homes and leave running the country up to men, whereas in 1999 the Gallup poll showed only 7 percent of respondents were willing to indicate that they would not vote for a qualified woman candidate of their party for president.

Finally, there are the findings from a 1991 survey commissioned by *Sports Illustrated* and conducted by Lieberman Research. Although at this point in U.S. political history, the most recent Gallup poll indicated that only 12 percent of Americans would not vote for a qualified woman of their own party for the presidency, fully 29 percent of male respondents and 19 percent of female respondents reported that they would be bothered by a woman president of the United States. The only other situation that bothered respondents more was a woman fighting on the front lines (which bothered 35 percent of male respondents and 32 percent of female respondents).

The conclusions that can be drawn from the variety of surveys and question wordings suggest that we must be cautious indeed about imputing reliability and validity to the Gallup poll numbers, when there is substantial evidence in other surveys that there is not nearly universal support for nor comfort among the American public for a woman president.

Gender Stereotypes

In addition to exploring the variety of public opinion measures that relate to the viability of a woman candidate for the presidency, it is helpful to examine persisting gender stereotypes that may impede the chances of success for a woman candidate for the presidency. Several scholarly studies have suggested that gender stereotyping of female candidates for political office is prevalent and can impede their success, especially for executive positions. In general, female candidates are stereotyped as *more* emotional, warm, and expressive and *less* tough, competent, and decisive than similarly situated male candidates. This attitude may prove to be a detriment to women seeking executive offices because there is a greater emphasis at the executive level (whether it be a state governor or the U.S. president) on instrumental rather than expressive traits. Women candidates are also perceived to be better able to handle "women's issues" such as education and health care, whereas male candidates are perceived to be better able to handle foreign affairs and the economy. This sexual division of competence has important consequences for women candidates seeking the presidency, because of the commander-in-chief responsibilities that attend to the role.

A poll commissioned by Deloitte and Touche and conducted by Roper Starch Worldwide revealed that American voters have prejudicial notions regarding the ability of a woman candidate to be tough. Their study showed that voters rank the following characteristics as most important in a president: (1) ability to lead in a crisis, (2) ability to make tough decisions, (3) trustworthiness, and (4) honesty. Fifty-one percent of respondents reported that a man would do a better job than a woman with regard to the ability to lead in a crisis. Thirty-eight percent of respondents reported that a man would be better able than a woman to make tough decisions. Women were favored by the electorate over men on trustworthiness and honesty.

[Elizabeth Dole] was trivialized on account of her sex by the conservative press and attacked on feminist issues by the liberal press.

Different Expectations of Women

Women candidates are often stereotyped as less competent than their male counterparts and this tendency is often reinforced by media coverage of women candidates that focus on their competence (or lack thereof) rather than their issue positions. Geraldine Ferraro was asked by reporters covering the 1984 presidential campaign about her hairstyle and her recipes for baking pies. Political commentary on Elizabeth Dole's bid in 1999 was such that her statements on the Kosovo [a region in the former Yugoslavia that was in the midst of ethnic warfare] situation were being overshadowed by her new haircut. Is it any wonder that women candidates are viewed as less credible than their male counterparts, given the biases apparent in press coverage and the lingering stereotypes that inform that coverage?

In a 1999 survey conducted by Fannie Mae Personal Finances Survey, respondents were asked to consider some common gender stereotypes and assess how much credence those stereotypes had in contemporary society. The responses indicate a recognition of some of the structural barriers that are impeding the progress of women in politics in general and the likelihood of a woman president in particular. A majority of respondents still subscribe to the notion that women are the primary caregivers for children as well as being primarily responsible for family social obligations. These responses show that not much has changed since Arlie Hochschild penned the well-known book, *The Second Shift: Working Parents and the Revolution at Home*, in 1989. Hochschild documented the fact that women tend to continue to maintain responsibility for child rearing and family obligations, even when they work as many hours per week, or more, than their male spouses. This double standard is especially evident in the media coverage of Massachusetts governor [from 2001 to 2003] Jane Swift. Governor Swift faced a barrage of criticism from both the left and the right for her decision to assume the governorship while continuing to work from home after the birth of her twins. . . .

In spite of the hype that hailed Elizabeth Dole as "the first credible woman candidate for president in history" and public opinion polls that showed that she was the third most popular person in the United States in 1998 (behind Bill and Hillary Clinton), Dole was unable to translate these qualities into the money necessary to continue her campaign. Analysts may disagree about the root causes of that failure, but an examination of media coverage of her campaign suggests that she battled with double binds [situations that present a person with two choices, one or both of which is penalizing] and backlash that may have contributed to the [small amount] of monetary support she was able to attract. Specifically, she was trivialized on account of her sex by the conservative press and attacked on feminist issues by the liberal press. The existence of public opinion polls showing that voters will not discriminate against a woman candidate did little to bolster her prospects for a successful bid for the presidency.

9

The U.S. Is Ready for a Woman President Who Projects a Feminine Image

Harriet Rubin

Harriet Rubin is the author of several books, most recently The Mona Lisa Stratagem: The Art of Women, Age and Power. *She is also a member of* USA Today's *editorial board.*

The U.S. is surely ready for a female president, but she won't be elected by trying to beat her male opponents at their own game. Instead, a female candidate must utilize mamisma—the power of her mature feminine qualities—to win over the nation. A female politician who exercises mamisma will make tough decisions like her male counterparts, but will frame them in more delicate, diplomatic language. Mamisma is especially powerful at this time, when most baby boomers, who make up a substantial segment of the electorate as well as those running for president, are over 50.

Is America ready to elect a female president? Of course we are. The most macho countries—Chile, Liberia, Germany— have recently elected women chief executives as symbols of change. So how can a female candidate in America tap the desire for change and avoid tripping on the stereotypes of gender prejudice? Can she appear presidential before we have a model of what female presidential power is?

Even the most powerful woman in politics can't yet hold her own against the most powerful man, it seems: When Bill and Hillary Clinton take a stage together, he makes her disappear, like a magician and his assistant. How then would she look on stage against Republican Sen. John McCain? She'll have to draw consistently on her "mamisma," not machismo. (After all, there are already too many alpha male Democrats in play.) And I'm not talking about machisma or female ferocity.

Mamisma is femininity defined by mature and maternal qualities. It lets a female candidate make men look like wimps while doing the taboo-dance, enticing people to fall in love with her.

The history of female leaders—queens, presidents, prime ministers—reveals that they sell mamisma hard. Israel's Golda Meir, for example, was no conventional object of desire. She seduced by making her desires plain, like any good mother. In *Munich*, Steven Spielberg's historically inspired account of Israel's plot to avenge the murder of its Olympic athletes, Meir takes five minutes to persuade a young man to abandon his pregnant wife and promising career for her own desperate mission. *That* is mamisma.

Mamisma works because after age 50, the laws of power change.

Take a look at Nancy Pelosi on the occasion of her swearing-in as House speaker earlier this month. She was engulfed by children. Is it accidental that the most famous medieval icons depict a Madonna embracing people whose faces beam with childlike innocence? It's no accident: It's mamisma.

The Beauty of Mamisma

Mamisma makes a strong woman appear ultimately nonthreatening—a quality we have not seen much in our youth-intoxicated culture.

But the world is changing. In France, never a bastion of powerful women, presidential candidate Segolene Royal, 53, is selling herself as the mother protector of the nation. She's taking a page from the playbook of great queens and women who behave like them.

After their youthful sexuality fades, mamisma women stand toe to toe with powerful men. They often refer to love and trust as bold alternatives to the hard edges of powers that be.

Queen Elizabeth I sought her subjects' love; she assumed she had their respect. Eleanor Roosevelt became a saint by insisting that the bottom line of government is love. By contrast, fired Hewlett-Packard CEO Carly Fiorina wore toughness like a set of dentures; she denied there was anything womanly about her. That is anti-mamisma.

Mamisma works because after age 50, the laws of power change. Law No. 1: After 50 a woman is praised for what she had been blamed for, as legendary anthropologist Margaret Mead believed. A woman's youthful mistakes may be reevaluated as signs of her bravery and vision.

Pritzker Prize–winning architect Zaha Hadid is today hailed for the same weird designs that earlier guaranteed her rejection by potential clients. Hillary Clinton might remind us that she was an early champion of health care reform and that she suffered attacks from all sides for it. Advisers may warn candidate Clinton to sidestep this chapter in her past. But if she were to forget this advice and follow the rules of mamisma, she would promote the fact that surviving the onslaught is her war-hero record. McCain, too, fought in an unpopular and losing war.

Power Shift Among Boomers

The second law of mamisma: The differences between Mars and Venus are fading in that sizable demographic, the baby boomers, the majority of whom are 50 or older. The sexes don't simply grow older at different speeds; men mature into femininity. While men become more emotional, rounder and softer in physique, women tend to bulk up. They are acknowledged as stronger than men after age 50 because "women age more slowly," says Eric Walsh, a geriatrician at Beth Israel Medical Center in New York. Women also become the primary caretakers, as men become physically the weaker sex. . . .

This is a new playing field. A mamisma woman will not gear her message to either gender, and she will wrap tough platforms in emotional language: To stand against sending more troops into Iraq, Pelosi would emotionalize the discussion, noting that Bush is trying not to appear weak, the criticism his father suffered.

Mamisma is anti-Machiavelli: seduction over divisiveness.

The third law of mamisma is that, as University of Chicago scholar Wendy Doniger points out, "Men would marry their mothers if they could." Why? Because they like being reminded that they are great. It's the ultra-maternal message. A female candidate would likewise remind the electorate that a golden future awaits—a message more seductive than better homeland security.

Seductive Politics

Queen Eleanor of Aquitaine in the 12th century led a revolt away from her John McCain-like husband, King Henry. While he was out selling people on crusades, Eleanor built a court of love which appealed to the child in everyone, the very opposite of her husband's vision. The youth of Europe joined her in droves. This extremely alternative vision let Eleanor escape the secondary roles as wife and helper, assert her independent sovereignty and dispense her own justice and her own patronage.

Eleanor's original ideal of courtly love informs our culture to this day. As in Eleanor's time, there is a constituency that wants to feel the love.

Mamisma is anti-Machiavelli: seduction over divisiveness. Is it a good thing? In a world run like a PlayStation war game, maturity would be a nice antidote. After all, who wouldn't want a return to the seriousness and authority of the Founding Fathers ... even if this time around, they just happen to be women?

10

U.S. Media's Depictions of Women Candidates Undermines Electability

Katie Heimer

Katie Heimer writes articles for the National Organization for Women.

As the first leading female contender for her party's presidential nomination, Senator Hillary Clinton receives substantial media attention. Such coverage generally either trivializes female politicians by focusing on their appearance and taste or uses gender stereotypes to question their leadership capabilities. For example, Clinton has been scrutinized for her choice of clothing, her figure, her interior design taste, and her ambition. Some journalists have not indulged in such sexist portrayals, and a few have criticized them outright, but for the most part, female politicians, especially Clinton, are subjected to questions and scrutiny that male politicians rarely face.

Do sexist stereotypes undermine the credibility of women politicians?

Although Senator Hillary Rodham Clinton (D-N.Y.) is not the first woman to run for president, she is the first to be the frontrunner for her party's nomination—which makes her both a media magnet and a media target. So NOW decided to take a look at how the media has covered Clinton in recent months. What we found spans the spectrum from intelligent and fair to appallingly sexist and pointless.

Examples of the latter fell into two main categories: those that trivialize female politicians by focusing on their clothing, hair, or taste in home decor, and those that position gender as her most important characteristic, playing on gender stereotypes in order to call into question her ability to provide strong, effective leadership.

Fortunately, these examples (yes, even some of them from female reporters) are countered by occasional displays of serious, responsible journalism. With sexism still deeply ingrained in our culture, it may be unrealistic to expect the media to be completely unbiased, but it is nonetheless important to approach the news with a vigilant and critical eye. . . .

When was the last time an opinion piece or cartoon commented on a male candidate's figure?

Female politicians have long struggled with a double standard: while being criticized or perceived as "soft" or "weak" if they come across as too traditionally feminine, they are also accused of being too "hard" or "strident" if they come off as assertive and powerful—traditionally masculine attributes. While these impossible standards are being subverted by successful women politicians such as new House Speaker Nancy Pelosi, many journalists don't seem to know what to do with strong women. These professionals, who should know better, often revert to old-fashioned sexism in describing women leaders (e.g., denigrating women for qualities, like aggressiveness or ambition, that are seen as positive attributes in men), scrutinizing their appearance, and concentrating on their roles as dutiful wives and mothers to the exclusion of their political accomplishments and records on the issues.

Pelosi and Clinton

Indeed, in Pelosi's first days as Speaker of the House, *The Washington Post*'s Style section ran an article on Nov. 10 dissecting her choice of clothing for her swearing in ceremony, in which writer Robin Givhan used the word "chic" to describe her appearance and claimed that "an Armani suit, for a woman, is a tool for playing with the boys without pretending to be one." As Annette Fuentes responded in a Feb. 13 [2007] *USA Today* opinion piece, "I would wager that Pelosi is one woman who doesn't play around with anyone." . . .

Clinton is no stranger to this kind of treatment from the press. An opinion article in *The Oklahoman* referenced her "frequent wearing of dark pants suits to conceal her bottom-heavy figure." Political cartoonist Nick Anderson created an animated cartoon which ran on the *Houston Chronicle* website featuring a curvaceous Clinton being asked, in the words of a popular song, "What you gonna do with all that junk? All that junk inside your trunk?" Without the accompanying drawing, one could have assumed that Anderson was referring [to] personal baggage, but the cartoon made clear that he was also making a sly dig at her shape. When was the last time an opinion piece or cartoon commented on a male candidate's figure?

Adding insult to injury, *The New York Times* published a Maureen Dowd piece (titled "Mama Hugs Iowa") on Jan. 31 [2007] charging that as First Lady, Clinton showed off "a long parade of unflattering outfits and unnervingly changing hairdos." So we not only have to hear about what she's wearing today, but what she wore (and how she styled her hair) in 1992. On Feb. 9 [2007], Reuters news agency reported fashion designer Donatella Versace's advice that "Hillary Clinton should tap into her feminine side and wear dresses and skirts instead of trousers."

A Florida paper, the *Sun-Sentinel*, chimed in on Feb. 16 [2007] with an article by Jura Koncius about Rosemarie Howe,

Clinton's interior designer, and how she helped the Senator decorate her Embassy Row house in a "comfortable yet elegant" scheme of "camel and coral."

Reality Check

Fuentes' *USA Today* op-ed provided a much-needed reality check, pointing out that "[w]omen in government stand out because of their strength, intellect, and ideas—not because of their hemlines. Yet here we are in 2007 still treating powerful women like a novelty." She expressed justifiable concern that "focusing on the clothing choices of serious female political players risks rendering them less than serious," something these reporters and editors know all too well. . . .

Chris Matthews, host of MSNBC's talk show Hardball, *has become notorious for his sexist remarks about [Senator Hillary] Clinton.*

As the reality of a female presidential frontrunner sinks in, the popular question seems to be, "Are we ready for a woman president?" This subject has inspired countless articles over the past several months, and Senator Clinton's name is scarcely mentioned without reference to her sex. This is to be expected—Clinton's gender does make her standing as Democratic frontrunner groundbreaking. However, journalists seem fixated on this one aspect, as if her gender wholly defined Clinton as a candidate, and not in a good way. On Jan. 22 [2007], ABC News anchor Charles Gibson, who reportedly refused to share the anchor desk with a woman, even asked Clinton skeptically, "Would you be in this position were it not for your husband?"

U.S. News & World Report's Gloria Borger accused her on Feb. 12 [2007] of using a so-called "mommy strategy" to soften her image and appeal to voters by playing up her role as a mother and wife, as if there's something suspect about a woman who is both a devoted parent and an accomplished politician. Others, grabbing for a clever play on words, have taken to rhyming "Obama" with "Mama," as in a Jan. 23 [2007] *Washington Post* editorial in which Eugene Robinson writes, "Obama, here comes Mama. And she doesn't play."

Influencing Public Opinion

In a Feb. 14 [2007] *Seattle Post-Intelligencer* column, Susan Paynter notes that the language used to discuss and refer to a candidate can affect public perception. Of recent modes of addressing Clinton, she suggests "for title, try Senator, not Mrs. or Mama."

Chris Matthews, host of MSNBC's talk show *Hardball*, has become notorious for his sexist remarks about Clinton. On Dec. 19, 2006, he charged that she was being coy about her political ambitions, comparing her to "a stripteaser saying she's flattered by the attention," and on two separate occasions—Jan. 25 and 26, 2007, he referred to her as an "uppity woman." In the aftermath of the congressional election on Nov. 8, 2006, he discussed her delivery of a "campaign barn burner speech," which, he suggested, was "harder to give for a woman," because it can "grate on some men when they listen to it, [like] fingers on a blackboard." Not content to level his sexist criticism on Clinton alone, he continued his rant, wondering how newly elected Speaker of the House Nancy Pelosi could "do the good fight against the president . . . without screaming? How does she do it without becoming grating?"

With so many reporters and columnists unable to see past Senator Clinton's gender, it was refreshing on Jan. 22 [2007] to see Salon.com's Tim Grieve point out the obvious: Clinton isn't running for "first woman president," she's "running for president, period."

Despite the rampant sexism in the media's treatment of female politicians, it's important to note that the issue that has attracted the most negative attention to Clinton has nothing to do with her gender, but relates to her Iraq war authorization vote in 2002. While the media's hounding of Clinton on this issue may be a bit extreme and counterproductive, it's worth noting that this is an attack that deals with a genuinely political issue, one that any male candidate might face (but hasn't so far).

11

The U.S. Is Ready for a Hispanic President

Ruben Navarrette Jr.

Ruben Navarrette Jr. is one of fewer than ten nationally syndicated Latino columnists in the U.S. He is an editorial writer and a member of the editorial board for the San Diego Union-Tribune.

New Mexico Governor Bill Richardson, the first Hispanic governor in the U.S., now seems determined to run for president. If elected, he would become the nation's first Hispanic president. Richardson has an abundance of political experience, and easily won reelection in New Mexico. Furthermore, in the midst of recent discussions about reform of U.S. immigration policy, Richardson's political and personal experiences would be an asset. At the same time, there has been a surge in anti–illegal immigrant sentiment that could work against him. When John F. Kennedy ran for president, many doubted that he could be elected because he was Catholic. But voters turned out to be less prejudiced than predicted, and there is reason to believe that today's voters may be as well.

I think he's going to do it—run for president. He'll have to take on fellow Democrats and the doubters who don't think the country is ready to break a 217-year tradition of sending only white males to the White House. They'll say he's not ready, either. Still, he's sure to generate lots of excitement because of his intelligence and charisma and the diversity he'd bring to a national ticket. And he also has a crossover appeal that transcends his own ethnic group.

I speak, of course, of New Mexico Gov. Bill Richardson. Who did you think I had in mind?

For the only Hispanic to hold one of the nation's governorships—and in a border state to boot—2008 will be either the best time to run for president, or the worst.

Put me in a third camp: It's about time. As in: It's about time a credible and qualified Hispanic made a serious bid for the presidential nomination of a major political party. With the highest ratio of Medal of Honor recipients relative to their percentage of the population, Hispanics have given much to this country. It's time they added a presidential candidate to the list.

Richardson would have to be considered a serious contender, no matter what his ethnicity. He's got the goods. Having served as a member of Congress, a Cabinet secretary and U.N. ambassador, Richardson also has the benefit of being a governor—in a Democratic field likely to be chock-full of senators, in a country where voters haven't elected a senator to the presidency since 1960. He won re-election this year with 69 percent of the vote.

And now to the question at hand: Is 2008 the best or the worst of times for Richardson to run for president?

Being of two worlds . . . [Richardson] is well-suited to introduce one to the other.

The Immigration Debate

The answer depends on what happens next year [2007], in Washington and around the country, with regard to one issue: immigration. A Democratic-controlled Congress might approve comprehensive reform that includes a path to legal residency for illegal immigrants.

Richardson has been pushing for just such an outcome, including lobbying members of Congress during a recent trip to Washington.

"I'm urging Democrats to take on immigration reform and to put it in the top tier of priorities, say in the top five, or else it'll never happen," he told me.

Richardson said his fear is that if Congress continues to duck this issue, local enforcement measures will take over, and then "it's going to get ugly."

One thing that Richardson thinks is already pretty ugly is anything resembling a wall along the border. He said so recently when he called on Congress to scuttle plans to construct 700 miles of new fencing.

"They passed this bill for this stupid fence, this horrendous symbol," he said. "It's not fully funded. It's so unpopular and not just with Hispanics. The border states hate it, business leaders hate it. It was this terrible vote in the last session, and it was just to convince voters they were serious, but it backfired on the extremists if you look at the election returns."

If immigration takes center stage, it could convince people that what they really need in 2008 is a president who is well-versed on the issue and all it entails.

That's Richardson. His mother was born in Mexico, and his father was an American businessman. Richardson was raised in Mexico City before going off to prep school in Massachusetts and then earning college and graduate degrees at Tufts University. Being of two worlds—bilingual, bicultural and binational—he is well-suited to introduce one to the other.

Beyond Bigotry?

On the other hand, if the anti–illegal immigrant backlash continues in many communities around the country—and continues to morph, as it has been, into an anti-Hispanic backlash—Richardson could spend half the campaign trying to convince those with closed minds and hair-trigger prejudices that his loyalty lies with the United States and not with Mexico.

This should ring a bell. In 1960, a Roman Catholic named John F. Kennedy spent a lot of time trying to convince Protestant voters that, if elected president, he wouldn't take orders from the Vatican. Nearly a half-century later, we can shake our heads at how ridiculous it was to even ask the question—one grounded in ignorance and bigotry.

Next year, if similar narrow-minded questions are asked surrounding the candidacy of Bill Richardson, let's hope that voters shake their heads again and conclude the same thing.

12

The U.S. Is Not Ready for an Asian American President

Emil Guillermo

Emil Guillermo's columns have appeared in the San Francisco Chronicle, Washington Post, Los Angeles Times, *and* USA Today. *He was the first non-white host of National Public Radio's news show,* All Things Considered.

The 2008 election has already brought forth a historical diversity of candidates, including an African American, a Latino, and a woman. But there are currently no Asian Americans running. Norm Mineta, the former congressman and cabinet member, has the credentials, but he says he's not interested in the presidency. Some Americans might have an easier time accepting an Asian American president than a Latino or black president, but with so many Americans still largely ignorant of Asian American issues and circumstances, the country is still far from ready.

Of the more than 25 people running, or considering a run for president [in 2008], diversity has emerged as key.

There's a black ([Barack] Obama), a woman (Hillary [Clinton]) and a Latino (Bill Richardson).

But that leaves us one short of a quorum for an anti-[Ku Klux] Klan rally.

I mean, really, where's the Asian American in this diversity love fest?

There isn't anyone.

Emil Guillermo, "Diversity Politics: Mineta for President?" *Asian Week*, vol. 3, no. 24, Feb. 2–8, 2007, p. 5. Reproduced by permission of the author.

Obama has a hard enough time convincing blacks he's black.

Hillary knows it takes a village, but I don't think that village is near Chinatown.

And Richardson has a long way to go before he outlives his role in the government's vicious attack on Wen Ho Lee [Taiwanese American scientist accused of stealing U.S. nuclear secrets for the Chinese government in 1999].

When the "minority" candidates have no ready ties to our community, it's pretty discouraging that we're left to consider such "stalwarts" as Duncan Hunter, John Edwards or Sam Brownback.

So where's the Asian American candidate?

Any takers? . . .

The reality is we may have to wait a long time.

Norm Mineta? The former secretary of both Commerce and Transportation? The former congressman and committee chairman from San Jose, and the former S.J. mayor?

In January, Mineta won the Presidential Medal of Freedom. It's the highest possible civilian honor. (We don't knight people in a democracy.) Wouldn't Mineta gladly trade in the hardware in exchange for a real presidential part?

Mineta thought I was crazy for asking.

"As the saying goes, 'If nominated I refuse to run, and if elected I refuse to serve,'" Mineta responded, citing a 19th century quote by Civil War General William Tecumseh Sherman.

"Be realistic," Mineta continued. "In January 2009 [the inaugural], I'll be 77."

Sounds like lucky numbers to me.

"Running? No," he said.

Dismiss it if you'd like. Asian Americans do revere more senior leaders. Age isn't the issue—look at China. But Mineta makes sense for America because he's no ideologue.

What America Needs

Mineta always had his heart, which is always in the right place. What's appealing about him is his style. It's exactly what this divided country needs right now. He knows that governing is a matter of working out solutions with the "other side."

You haven't seen a lot of that in Washington during the Bush Administration.

What kind of world is it where you can have a Filipino in the Oval Office and in the presidential pantry?

And when you have it's been because of Mineta. Bush tabbed him to be the Democrat in his Republican cabinet for a reason. Mineta has long been the person who has reached across the aisle.

He'd have the statesmanship and the ability to be the chief executive.

But at this point, desire and ambition are worth more than experience or talent.

And Mineta's desire isn't to wipe up after the president.

"I'm enjoying life now," said Mineta, who is vice-chairman of Hill and Knowlton, the huge international public relations conglomerate.

Which brings us back to one of my observations about the presidency: Who'd want to inherit the colossal mess that is Iraq? . . .

I could use the income, if not the headache.

No. Not me.

But many others are saying "Me, me, me."

That's what happens when the qualifications devalue experience, and put a premium on one's willingness to be an "agent of change."

It's easy enough to declare. And so everyone is.

That's both good and bad for democracy. Good because it shows even lightweight Republicans like Duncan Hunter can throw their hat into the ring.

Bad because, a wide-open race usually leads to a confused, unwieldy mess. But perhaps not bad enough to want to bring back the monarchy. . . .

That still leaves us without an Asian American candidate.

The reality is we may have to wait a long time. Winning the presidency is a bit like Everest. (Those inaugurals are cold!) Making the trek takes its toll.

A Long Way Off

Perhaps the next risk-taking APA [Asian Pacific American] isn't a second-generation Ivy League grad, one who plays it safe and becomes an investment banker. But maybe it's the risk-taking APA, the immigrant-turned-pol, now working in the trenches at the grassroots level. Maybe it's one of the former refugees who now finds himself or herself in state and local politics in California?

We're still a generation, and a change in the law away. (Immigrants as president are still verboten, unless [California governor and Austrian native Arnold] Schwarzenegger makes it to the presidency before us.)

There are, however, at least two Asian Americans that do come to mind. Former governor of Washington, Gary Locke. Currently in Seattle practicing law, Locke would be a good standard bearer.

And since presidents tend to be governors first, I'd even toss in former Hawai'i Governor Ben Cayetano's name.

What kind of world is it where you can have a Filipino in the Oval Office and in the presidential pantry?

That, my friend, is democracy!

But what about electability?

You've heard all the arguments on whether America is ready to elect a black or a woman or a Latino. But what about Asian American?

Frankly, I'd say an Asian American would have less trouble appealing to a non-diversity oriented white who has trouble with a Latino or black.

After all, they eat our food, drive our cars and rent our kung fu movies.

Still, you know there will be a moment, maybe in Iowa, or the South, when someone will innocently ask an Asian American candidate, "What country are you from?"

That's how you know America isn't really ready yet.

13

The U.S. Is Ready for a Mormon Presidential Candidate

David E. Campbell and J. Quin Monson

David E. Campbell is an assistant professor of political science at University of Notre Dame. J. Quin Monson is an assistant professor of political science at Brigham Young University.

Republican Presidential candidate Mitt Romney's Mormonism has already been the root of open criticism by political pundits, as well as polls showing many Americans would be reluctant to vote for him. The fears expressed about Romney's presidency are the same as those expressed about John F. Kennedy, the first Catholic president, when he ran in 1960. While the Mormon Church, like the Vatican, does issue policy statements, an elected official who is Mormon is not bound to follow them. Romney will only have a chance of winning the election if he makes this clear to the American voters. He must be forthright with the voters about his religious faith, just as Kennedy was.

Should Americans fear Mitt Romney because he is a Mormon? In spite of what some political pundits have recently argued, the answer is a resounding no.

Should Romney fear how some Americans will react to his religion? Unfortunately, recent polls say yes. But just like another Massachusetts politician who faced questions about his religion, namely, John F. Kennedy, Romney can, and should, tackle uneasiness about his religion head-on—sooner rather than later.

David E. Campbell and J. Quin Monson, "The Religious Test," *USA Today*, Jan. 22, 2007, p. 9A. Reproduced by permission of the authors.

Romney has not yet officially announced his plans to run for the Republican nomination, yet the darts have already begun to fly. In fact, some critics have argued that Romney should not be elected solely because of his membership in the Church of Jesus Christ of Latter-day Saints (LDS):

Writing in *Slate*, columnist Jacob Weisberg says that if Romney truly believes in his religion, "I don't want him running the country."

Damon Linker, in *The New Republic*, says voters should reject Romney on religious grounds. Echoing precisely the same concerns raised about Kennedy's Catholicism, Linker argues that a Mormon president would be controlled by his church's hierarchy. In his words, "Would it not be accurate to say that under a President Romney, the Church of Jesus Christ of Latter-day Saints would truly be in charge of the country?" Actually, no, it would not be accurate, any more than it was accurate to say that Kennedy would take orders from the Vatican. And neither would it be accurate to accuse the LDS church of pulling the strings of other prominent Mormon politicians, such as Senate Majority Leader Harry Reid, D-Nev., Sen. Gordon Smith, R-Ore., the late Rep. Mo Udall, D-Ariz., and numerous others.

Many voters are simply reflecting the fact that Mormonism is unfamiliar to them.

Church and State

It is true that, like many religious groups, the LDS church occasionally makes policy pronouncements, as it did last June [2006] in support of a federal constitutional amendment banning gay marriage. However, this kind of political activity has not served to constrain Mormon elected officials. Reid, at the time the Senate minority leader, led the opposition to the amendment. In response to a reporter's question about his open opposition to the LDS church's public position, his press secretary Sharyn Stein said that the church had asked members to express their opinions on the issue, so her boss was doing so "loudly and repeatedly on the Senate floor."

A President Romney would have the same autonomy to speak and act independently of his church.

Romney's challenge, however, is to make this clear to the American public. It is here that the parallel to Catholicism is instructive.

John F. Kennedy was not the first Catholic to run for president. That distinction belongs to Gov. Al Smith, D-N.Y., who, after winning the Democratic nomination in 1928, faced outright hostility to his Catholicism and suffered an ignominious defeat at the polls. The anti-Catholic bigotry that Smith confronted was in the living memory of many Democrats as Kennedy began his bid for the presidency. In an era when primaries were non-binding and often ignored by the leading candidates, Kennedy entered the West Virginia primary to show that a Catholic could win in a heavily Baptist state and thus settle the "Catholic question." He won the primary and the nomination. But still doubts lingered in the minds of the electorate about his religion.

To put those doubts to rest, Kennedy marched into the proverbial lion's den and delivered a speech to Protestant ministers in Houston. That speech is a classic appeal for religious tolerance. In it, Kennedy declared, "I do not speak for my church on public matters, and the church does not speak for me."

It is wrong to reject Romney because of his faith, just as it was wrong to reject Kennedy for his.

Put Concerns to Rest

Similarly, enough Americans have doubts about Romney's religion that he should not wait for the primaries to tackle the

"Mormon question." Recent polls find that about four out of 10 Americans say that they are unwilling to vote for a Mormon. We suspect that many voters are simply reflecting the fact that Mormonism is unfamiliar to them; it is natural to be uneasy with the unknown. However, Romney's own election in Massachusetts as well as the elections of Gordon Smith, Rep. Ernest Istook, R-Okla., and former U.S. Representative Richard Swett, D-N.H., demonstrate that voters outside the Mountain West, where Mormons are most heavily concentrated, can become comfortable with Mormon candidates from across the political spectrum.

The heavy scrutiny focused on presidential candidates, even this early in the campaign, and the unease of some voters with a Mormon president, means that Romney should do now what Kennedy waited until the fall of 1960 to do. Romney needs to take a page from the Kennedy playbook and address his religion forthrightly, in a high-profile venue.

At a time when religion and politics are increasingly intertwined, it would be an opportunity to remind all Americans why the wall between church and state has served the country well.

Whatever issues voters might have with Mormonism, it is wrong to reject Romney because of his faith, just as it was wrong to reject Kennedy for his, or to disqualify today's Catholic politicians, such as Sen. John Kerry, D-Mass., and House Speaker Nancy Pelosi, D-Calif., for theirs. It is no different from dismissing Sen. Hillary Clinton, D-N.Y., because of her gender or Sen. Barack Obama, D-Ill., because of his race.

No Religious Test

This is not an endorsement of Romney—we leave it to the voters to decide whether he deserves to be president. Rather, we endorse the spirit of Article VI in the Constitution, which states that there should be no religious test for public office.

Kennedy captured that spirit well in 1960 when he said: "While this year it may be a Catholic against whom the finger of suspicion is pointed, in other years it has been—and may someday be again—a Jew, or a Quaker, or a Unitarian, or a Baptist."

Or even a Mormon.

14

The U.S. Is Not Ready for a Mormon President

Jacob Weisberg

Jacob Weisberg is editor of the online magazine Slate. *He has written about politics for* Newsweek *and the* New Republic, *among other publications.*

Despite his political qualifications, Republican presidential candidate Mitt Romney is already facing scrutiny from the American public because of his Mormonism, and this skepticism is justified. Refusing to vote for a candidate of a certain religion is different from not voting for a candidate because of his or her race or gender; a candidate's religious beliefs demonstrate how he or she sees the world. While all religious beliefs are irrational to some extent, Mormonism is much more transparently fraudulent than older religions like Christianity and Judaism. Romney may not take his orders from Mormon Church doctrine if elected, but at this point, Americans have no reason to believe he wouldn't.

Someone who refuses to consider voting for a woman as president is rightly deemed a sexist. Someone who'd never vote for a black person is a racist. But are you a religious bigot if you wouldn't cast a ballot for a believing Mormon?

The issue arises with Massachusetts Gov. Mitt Romney's as-yet-undeclared bid for the 2008 Republican nomination. Romney would not be the first member of the Church of Jesus Christ of Latter-day Saints to run for the nation's highest office. He follows Orrin Hatch (2000); Mo Udall (1976); his father, George Romney (1968); and not least of all Joseph Smith, who ran in 1844 on a platform of "theodemocracy," abolition, and cutting congressional pay. Despite a strong showing in the Nauvoo straw poll, Smith didn't play much better nationally than Hatch did, and had to settle for the Mormon-elected post of King of the Kingdom of Heaven.

With his experience as a successful businessman, Olympic organizer, and governor, Romney has a better chance, but he may still have to overcome a tall religious hurdle. According to a recent Rasmussen poll, only 38 percent of Americans say they'd definitely consider voting for a Mormon for president. Yet many analysts think LDS membership is not an insuperable obstacle. Various evangelical sects continue to view Mormonism as heretical, non-Christian, or even satanic. But because of their shared faith in social conservatism, evangelical leaders seem open to supporting Romney. As far apart as they are theologically, Mormons and evangelical Christians may have more in common with each other anthropologically than they do with secular Americans watching *Big Love* on HBO. The remaining skepticism on the far right seems to have more to do with doubt about whether Romney has truly and forever ditched his previously expressed moderate views on abortion and gay rights.

I wouldn't vote for someone who truly believed in the founding whoppers of Mormonism.

Religious Views Are Relevant

But if he gets anywhere in the primaries, Romney's religion will become an issue with moderate and secular voters—and rightly so. Objecting to someone because of his religious beliefs is not the same thing as prejudice based on religious heritage, race, or gender. Not applying a religious test for public office means that people of all faiths are allowed to run—

not that views about God, creation, and the moral order are inadmissible for political debate. In George W. Bush's case, the public paid far too little attention to the role of religion in his thinking. Many voters failed to appreciate that while Bush's religious beliefs may be moderate Methodist ones, he was someone who relied on his faith immoderately, as an alternative to rational understanding of complex issues.

Nor is it chauvinistic to say that certain religious views should be deal breakers in and of themselves. There are millions of religious Americans who would never vote for an atheist for president, because they believe that faith is necessary to lead the country. Others, myself included, would not, under most imaginable circumstances, vote for a fanatic or fundamentalist—a Hassidic Jew who regards Rabbi Menachem Schneerson [former leader of the Chabad-Lubavitch Hasidic movement] as the Messiah, a Christian literalist who thinks that the Earth is less than 7,000 years old, or a Scientologist who thinks it is haunted by the souls of space aliens sent by the evil lord Xenu. Such views are disqualifying because they're dogmatic, irrational, and absurd. By holding them, someone indicates a basic failure to think for himself or see the world as it is.

Romney has never publicly indicated any distance from church doctrine.

Mormonism Is Different

By the same token, I wouldn't vote for someone who truly believed in the founding whoppers of Mormonism. The LDS church holds that Joseph Smith, directed by the angel Moroni, unearthed a book of golden plates buried in a hillside in Western New York in 1827. The plates were inscribed in "reformed" Egyptian hieroglyphics—a nonexistent version of the ancient language that had yet to be decoded. If you don't know the story, it's worth spending some time with Fawn

Brodie's wonderful biography *No Man Knows My History*. Smith was able to dictate his "translation" of the Book of Mormon first by looking through diamond-encrusted decoder glasses and then by burying his face in a hat with a brown rock at the bottom of it. He was an obvious con man. Romney has every right to believe in con men, but I want to know if he does, and if so, I don't want him running the country.

One may object that all religious beliefs are irrational— what's the difference between Smith's "seer stone" and the virgin birth or the parting of the Red Sea? But Mormonism is different because it is based on such a transparent and recent fraud. It's Scientology plus 125 years. Perhaps Christianity and Judaism are merely more venerable and poetic versions of the same. But a few eons makes a big difference. The world's greater religions have had time to splinter, moderate, and turn their myths into metaphor. The Church of Latter-day Saints is expanding rapidly and liberalizing in various ways, but it remains fundamentally an orthodox creed with no visible reform wing.

Romney's Principles

It may be that Mitt Romney doesn't take Mormon theology at face value. His flip-flopping on gay rights and abortion to suit the alternative demands of a Massachusetts gubernatorial election and a Republican presidential primary suggests that he's a man of flexible principles—which in this context might be regarded as encouraging. But Romney has never publicly indicated any distance from church doctrine. He is an "elder" who performed missionary service in France as a young man and did not protest the church's overt racism and priestly discrimination before it was abolished in 1978. He usually tries to defuse the issue with the tired jokes about polygamy, or cries foul and insists that his religious views are "private." That they may be, but if he's running for president, they concern the rest of us, as well.

15

The U.S. Is Not Ready for a Jewish President

Jeffrey H. Birnbaum

Jeffrey H. Birnbaum is a columnist for the Washington Post *as well as a political analyst on Fox News Channel and a regular panelist on PBS's* Washington Week. *He has written for* Fortune, Time, *and the* Wall Street Journal, *where he was a White House correspondent.*

Despite his qualifications and popularity, Connecticut Senator and 2004 presidential candidate Joseph Lieberman is behind his Democratic rivals in the polls. One major but rarely acknowledged factor is his religion. Americans would be less comfortable with a Jewish president, especially an Orthodox Jewish president, than many think. In addition to reports that anti-Semitism has increased in recent years, Lieberman, or any other Jewish candidate, will face more scrutiny when it comes to his foreign policy positions. Although there are plenty of Jewish legislators in Washington, it is doubtful that America would elect a Jewish president at this point in time.

Joe Lieberman should be the hands-down front-runner for President among Democrats [in the 2004 election]. He came within a chad's width of being elected Vice President [in the 2000 election] and is better known than any of his eight rivals. But polls show that the Connecticut Senator is behind in such key states as Iowa and New Hampshire, and political insiders don't give him much chance of winning the nomination. There are several reasons for this, but one big one is rarely discussed in public: Lieberman is a Jew.

I hate to write those words. I'm Jewish and—I admit it—I like Lieberman. He's wry and wise in the right proportions and willing to defy his party on matters of principle. He's a good man. But he is also a member of a tiny and long-scorned minority. Plenty of people won't vote for him simply because of his religion, whether they admit it or not. And, I'm ashamed to say, lots of Jews are reluctant to back him as well. After suffering years of discrimination, they fear that having too prominent a Jew on the national scene could spark an outbreak of anti-Semitism.

That may come as a shock, given what a hit Lieberman was in 2000. The novelty of having a Jew on the ticket for the first time was widely considered a boon for the Democrats and helped revive Al Gore's lackluster campaign. Many experts asserted that Lieberman's devout beliefs attracted voters, particularly fundamentalist Christians who were otherwise Republican stalwarts. If there was strong anti-Jewish feeling, it didn't show up in the polls.

Democratic leaders say they don't hear much talk about anti-Semitism—except among Jews. And among them, there's a lot.

But Lieberman was running for Veep back then. Now, as a candidate for the top spot, he faces much tougher scrutiny. Issues that barely mattered in 2000 can be important. Such as this basic fact: Only 2% of Americans are Jewish. If you live in or near a big city like New York or Los Angeles, that sounds too low. But in fact, to most Americans, Jews are strangers. Lieberman's form of the religion, Orthodox Judaism, is especially unfamiliar. He stops whatever he's doing three times a day to chant his prayers. He occasionally carries kosher meals on the road. Friday night and Saturday, to observe the Sabbath, he doesn't work, ride in a car, or turn on lights (except in an emergency). Having grown up in an Orthodox family, I understand and even admire those acts, but I doubt my view will be widely shared.

Anti-Semitism

The nonpartisan Anti-Defamation' League (ADL) published a survey last year showing that anti-Jewish sentiment was on the rise. It found that 17% of Americans, or about 35 million adults, "hold views about Jews that are unquestionably anti-Semitic." That represented an increase from 12% in 1998. What is more, the ADL found, 35% of African-Americans held strong anti-Semitic opinions. Black votes are significant in several early Democratic primaries, particularly South Carolina, where they'll make up a third to half of the electorate. Rural white voters in the state might also think twice about Lieberman, says Scott Huffmon, a political scientist at Winthrop University in Rock Hill, S.C. "In a place where the Confederate battle flag is so prominent, [Lieberman's] religion will be in the minds of many people." Right now, Lieberman is slightly ahead of his rivals in South Carolina polls—and in nationwide polls as well—but that's mostly because of name recognition. He's significantly behind "undecided."

Whether a Jew can reach the White House is very much in question.

Democratic leaders say they don't hear much talk about anti-Semitism—except among Jews. And among them, there's a lot. "There's a sense of pride, but at the same time there's significant nervousness," says Abraham Foxman, national director of the ADL. "If Lieberman makes a mistake, will it redound to the detriment of the Jewish community?"

Foreign Policy

Lieberman also faces trouble on foreign policy. Some Jews worry that if one of their own were President, he would have to restrain his pro-Israel impulses to avoid criticism. Says one Jewish pollster who works for Democrats: "There are a lot of Jews who are saying 2000 was a great time to have a Jewish Vice President, but 2004 seems like a bad time for a Jewish President."

Indeed, President Bush's steadfast support of Israel has inspired a growing number of Jews, who have traditionally voted heavily Democratic, to consider backing the GOP in the next election. That trend has hurt Lieberman where it counts. The largest surprise of the political season has been that Lieberman is trailing his Democratic opponents on the money front. His donations lag behind those of John Edwards of North Carolina, John Kerry of Massachusetts, and Richard Gephardt of Missouri. Lieberman's aides say that he's catching up fast and assert that Jewish money is rolling in just fine. But official Washington has noticed the problem and is discounting Lieberman's chances.

Then again, Americans' open-mindedness has been underestimated before. John F. Kennedy was supposed to lose the presidential election in 1960 because he was Catholic. Instead he broke a religious barrier. The Democratic field for President this year [2003] is actually chock full of Jewishness. Kerry recently revealed that his paternal grandparents were Austrian Jews who converted to Catholicism. Former Governor Howard Dean of Vermont has spoken at length about his Jewish wife, Judy, and his two Jewish-raised children. And if Congress is a guide, Jews are more than welcome. Capitol Hill has a record number of Jewish lawmakers: 11 in the Senate and 24 in the House.

But whether a Jew can reach the White House is very much in question. And that I sincerely regret.

Organizations to Contact

The editors have compiled the following list of organizations concerned with the issues debated in this book. The descriptions are derived from materials provided by the organizations. All have publications or information available for interested readers. The list was compiled on the date of publication of the present volume; the information provided here may change. Be aware that many organizations take several weeks or longer to respond to inquiries, so allow as much time as possible.

American-Arab Anti-Discrimination Committee (ADC)
1732 Wisconsin Ave, NW, Washington, DC   20007
(202) 244-2990 • fax: (202) 244-7968
Web site: www.adc.org

The American-Arab Anti-Discrimination Committee is a grassroots civil rights organization committed to defending the rights of people of Arab descent. It combats negative stereotyping of Arabs in the media, promotes a balanced U.S. Mideast policy, and offers legal services in cases of discrimination and defamation. It published the *Report on Hate Crimes and Discrimination Against Arab Americans: The Post-September 11 Backlash* and publishes the *ADC Times* as well as periodic Action Alerts.

American Jewish Committee (AJC)
165 East 56 Street, New York, NY   10022
(212) 751-4000 • fax: (212) 891-6710
Web site: www.ajc.org

The American Jewish Committee is an international think tank and advocacy organization established in 1906 with the goal of promoting pluralistic and democratic societies. Its key areas of focus include combating anti-Semitism and other forms of bigotry; promoting pluralism and democratic values, and supporting Israel's quest for peace and security. It publishes the annual *American Jewish Year Book, AJC in the Courts,* the *Annual Survey of American Jewish Opinion,* and many other publications.

Anti-Defamation League (ADL)

P.O. Box 96226, Washington, DC   20090-6226
(202) 452-8310 • fax: (202) 296-2371
e-mail: washington-dc@adl.org
Web site: www.adl.org

Founded in 1913, the Anti-Defamation League's mission is to combat defamation of the Jewish people and promote fair and just treatment for all people. It publishes the following newsletters: *Connections, Headlines, International Report, On Guard,* and *Terrorism Update,* among other publications.

Arab American Institute

1600 K Street, NW, Suite 601, Washington, DC   20006
(202) 429-9210 • fax: (202) 429-9214
Web site: www.aaiusa.org

The Arab American Institute (AAI) is a nonprofit organization that represents Arab American policy and community interests. AAI also promotes Arab American participation in the U.S. electoral system. It publishes an Annual Roster of Arab Americans in Public Service as well as the *AAI Congressional Scorecard.*

Asian American Institute

4753 North Broadway, Suite 904, Chicago, IL   60640
(773) 271-0899 • fax: (773) 271-1982
e-mail: aai@aaichicago.org
Web site: www.aaichicago.org

The Asian American Institute is a nonprofit organization established in 1992. Its mission is to empower the Asian American community through advocacy, research, education, and coalition building. Among its publications are: *Asian American*

Compass: A Guide to Navigating the Community, A Comprehensive Guide to the Asian American Community, and *Asian American Political Empowerment Initiative.*

Center for American Women in Politics
Eagleton Institute of Politics
New Brunswick, NJ   08901-8557
(732) 932-9384 • fax: (732) 932-0014
Web site: www.cawp.rutgers.edu

The Center for American Women and Politics (CAWP) is a center for research, education, and public service. It seeks to educate the public about women's participation in politics and government, as well as promote such participation. The Center publishes two series of reports: *The Impact of Women in Office* and *Bringing More Women into Public Office* as well as Fact Sheets about Women in Elective and Appointive Office, among other publications.

Emily's List
1120 Connecticut Avenue NW, Suite 1100
Washington, DC   20036
(202) 326-1400 • fax: (202) 326-1415
e-mail: information@emilyslist.org
Web site: www.emilyslist.org

Emily's List is an organization founded in 1985 dedicated to electing pro-choice Democratic women to federal, state, and local office. It publishes *Essential ELements*, which provides political news online, and *Women's Monitor*, which provides periodic reports on key issues for women as well as women's voting patterns.

Leadership Education for Asian Pacifics, Inc. (LEAP)
327 E. 2nd Street, Suite 226, Los Angeles, CA   90012
(213) 485-1422 • fax: (213) 485-0050
e-mail: leap@leap.org
Web site: www.leap.org

The mission of LEAP is to achieve full participation and equality for Asian Americans and Pacific Islanders in the U.S. It does this through developing leaders, educating the public, and empowering communities. LEAP's publications include the online newsletter, *LEAP Connections*, *The State of Asian Pacific America* series, *In Support of Civil Rights: Taking on the Initiative*, and others.

League of United Latin American Citizens (LULAC)
2000 L Street NW, Suite 610, Washington, DC   20036
(202) 833-6130 • fax: (202) 833-6135
Web site: www.lulac.org

LULAC, the largest and oldest Hispanic organization in the United States, advances the economic conditions, civil rights, and political power of Hispanic Americans through community-based programs. Its publications include the magazine *LULAC News* and the *LULAC Civil Rights Manual*.

League of Women Voters (LWV)
1730 M Street NW, Suite 1000, Washington, DC   20036-4508
(202) 429-1965 • fax: (202) 429-0854
Web site: www.lwv.org

The League of Women Voters is a nonpartisan political organization founded in 1920 to encourage informed and active participation in government. It does not support or oppose political candidates. The League of Women Voters publishes a triennial magazine, *National Voter*, the monthly electronic newsletter, *LeaguE-Voice*, as well as resource guides such as *Observing Your Government in Action*.

National Association for the Advancement of Colored People (NAACP)
4805 Mt. Hope Drive, Baltimore, MD   21215
(410) 580-5777
Web site: www.naacp.org

The NAACP is the country's oldest civil rights organization. Founded in 1909, its mission is to ensure the political, educational, social, and economic equality of all people and to eliminate racial hatred and discrimination. The NAACP publishes the bimonthly magazine *The Crisis* as well as numerous other publications on the topics of health, education, and economic empowerment.

National Council of La Raza
Raul Yzaguirre Building, Washington, DC   20036
(202) 785-1670
Web site: www.nclr.org

The National Council of La Raza (NCLR) is the largest national Hispanic civil rights organization in the United States. NCLR seeks to expand opportunities for Hispanic Americans through applied research, policy analysis, and advocacy. Among its numerous publications are *The Latino Electorate: Profiles and Trends, Poll Summary of Latino Voters for 2006 Elections, A Pocket Guide on Six Important Issues for Latino Voters,* and *The NCLR Voter Guide.*

National Urban League (NUL)
120 Wall Street, 8th Floor, New York, NY   10005
(212) 558-5300 • fax: (212) 344-5332
e-mail: info@nul.org
Web site: www.nul.org

The National Urban League is devoted to helping African Americans to secure economic and political power, and civil rights. Headquartered in New York City, the National Urban League has over 100 local affiliates that provide services to more than 2 million people through its programs, advocacy, and research. Its publications include *The State of Black America,* published annually, as well as the magazines *Opportunity Journal* and *Urban Influence.*

Project Vote Smart
1 Common Ground, Philipsburg, MT   59858
(406) 859-8683
Web site: www.vote-smart.org

Project Vote Smart is a nonprofit organization that provides information to the public about elected officials and candidates. It does not accept funding from corporations, political action committees (PACs), or partisan political organizations. Project Vote Smart publishes *The Voter's Self-Defense Manual*, *The Reporter's Source Book*, and *The Project Vote Smart Video*.

The White House Project
434 West 33rd Street, 8th Floor, New York, NY   10001
(212) 261-4400 • fax: (212) 904-1296
Web site: www.thewhitehouseproject.org

The White House Project is a nonprofit, nonpartisan organization with the goal of expanding American women's political leadership, all the way up to the presidency. The organization supports women and those issues that it sees as encouraging women's success, such as health care and economic stability. It publishes the blog *CHANGE Everything*.

Bibliography

Books

David E. Campbell — *Why We Vote: How Schools and Communities Shape Our Civic Life*, Princeton, NJ: Princeton University Press, 2006.

Susan J. Carroll, Ed. — *Women and American Politics: New Questions, New Directions*, New York: Oxford University Press, 2003.

Susan J. Carroll and Richard L. Fox, Eds. — *Gender and Elections: Shaping the Future of American Politics*, New York: Cambridge University Press, 2005.

Benjamin DeMott — *Junk Politics: The Trashing of the American Mind*, New York: Nation Books, 2003.

Kathleen A. Dolan — *Voting for Women: How the Public Evaluates Women Candidates*, Boulder, CO: Westview Press, 2003.

Richard J. Ellis and Michael Nelson, Eds. — *Debating the Presidency: Conflicting Perspectives on the American Executive*, Washington, DC: CQ Press, 2006.

Michael A. Genovese and Lori Cox Han, Eds. — *The Presidency and the Challenge of Democracy*, New York: Palgrave Macmillan, 2006.

Kim Geron — *Latino Political Power*, Boulder, CO: Lynn Riener Publishers, 2005.

Nichola D. Gutgold — *Paving the Way for Madam President*, Lanham, MD: Lexington Books, 2006.

Charles O. Jones — *The American Presidency: A Very Short Introduction*, New York: Oxford University Press, 2007.

Norman Kelley — *The Head Negro in Charge Syndrome: The Dead End of Black Politics*, New York: Nation Books, 2004.

Jennifer L. Lawless and Richard L. Fox — *It Takes a Candidate: Why Women Don't Run for Office*, New York: Cambridge University Press, 2005.

Sidney M. Milkis and Michael Nelson — *The American Presidency: Origins and Development, 1776–2002*, 4th ed., Washington, DC: CQ Press, 2003.

Michael Nelson, Ed. — *The Presidency and the Political System*, 8th ed., Washington, DC: CQ Press, 2005.

James P. Pfiffner — *The Modern Presidency*, Belmont, CA: Wadsworth Publishing, 2007.

James P. Pfiffner and Roger H. Davidson — *Understanding the Presidency*, 4th ed., New York: Longman, 2006.

Joseph August Pika and John Anthony Maltese — *The Politics of the Presidency*, 6th ed., Washington, DC: CQ Press, 2005.

Jorge Ramos — *The Latino Wave: How Hispanics Are Transforming Politics in America*, New York: Rayo, 2004.

Dick Stoken — *The Great Game of Politics: Why We Elect, Whom We Elect*, New York: Forge Books, 2004.

Sue Thomas and Clyde Wilcox, Eds. — *Women and Elective Office: Past, Present, and Future*, 2nd ed., New York: Oxford University Press, 2005.

Ronald W. Walters — *Freedom Is Not Enough: Black Voters, Black Candidates, and American Presidential Politics*, Lanham, MD: Rowman & Littlefield, 2005.

Robert P. Watson, Ann Gordon, Eds. — *Anticipating Madame President*, Boulder, CO: Lynne Rienner Publishers, Inc., 2003.

Stephen J. Wayne — *Is This Any Way to Run a Democratic Election?*, 3rd ed., Washington, DC: CQ Press, 2007.

Periodicals

Jonathan Alter — "Is America Ready?" *Newsweek*, Dec. 25, 2006.

Marcia Angell — "Hillary Clinton and the Glass Ceiling," *The Boston Globe*, Feb. 19, 2007.

Dan Balz — "Race and Gender Make Democrats' Field Historic," *Washington Post*, Jan. 17, 2007.

Gerald Bazer — "Break U.S. Mold for President," *Toledo Blade*, Jan. 15, 2005.

Gloria Borger — "The Mommy Factor," *U.S. News and World Report*, Feb. 12, 2007.

John H. Bunzel — "Is America Ready for a Mormon President?" *The Boston Globe*, Feb. 19, 2006.

Tony Castro — "Richardson Walks Tightrope as Top Latino Candidate," *LA Daily News*, Apr. 14, 2007.

Ellis Cose — "A Race Away from the Past; He Isn't a Product of the Civil-Rights Movement. Maybe That's Why Obama's Got a Chance," *Newsweek*, Jan. 29, 2007.

David E. Drew and Hedley Burrell — "Will Another White Male Be Elected President in 2008?" *Christian Science Monitor*, Jan. 5, 2007.

Geraldine Ferraro and Rev. Jesse L. Jackson — "What We Learned the Hard Way; Two Trailblazers Recall Their White House Runs, and How America Has Changed Since Then," *Newsweek*, Dec. 25, 2006.

Vicki Haddock — "Are We Ready for a Woman President?" *San Francisco Chronicle*, Apr. 29, 2007.

Michael Hill — "Madam President?" *Baltimore Sun*, May 6, 2007.

Jeff Jacoby — "We'd Elect a Black President? Old News," *The Boston Globe*, Dec. 27, 2006.

Mel Levine — "Is America Ready for a Jewish President?" *Jewish Journal*, June 20, 2003.

Jeremy I. Levitt   "Is America Really Ready for Obama?" *Chicago Sun-Times*, Jan. 20, 2007.

Damon Linker   "The Big Test," *New Republic*, Jan. 1, 2007.

Damon Linker   "A Bigger Tent," *Slate*, Oct. 11, 2006.

Kate Nash   "Analysis: Is America Ready for 'Presidente Richardson'?" *Albuquerque Tribune*, Jan. 18, 2007.

Ruben Navarrette Jr.   "A Hispanic Who Would Be President," *San Diego Union-Tribune*, Jan. 24, 2007.

Clarence Page   "Doubt Biggest Hurdle for '08 Diversity Trifecta," *Chicago Tribune*, Jan. 28, 2007.

Katha Pollitt   "HRC: Can't Get No Respect," *The Nation*, Nov. 20, 2006.

Tracie Powell   "Is America Ready to Elect a Black President?" *Diverse*, Jan. 21, 2007.

Tim Rutten   "Romney's Religious Rights," *LA Times*, Jan. 13, 2007.

Mary Sanchez   "The Gender Ceiling in National Politics," *Sacramento Bee*, Apr. 8, 2007.

Luiza Ch. Savage   "U.S. Voters Seem Ready to Elect a Black President. Barack Obama Is Counting on It," *Maclean's*, Feb. 5, 2007.

Carol M. Swain and Rev. Al Sharpton "Is America Ready for a Black President?" *Ebony*, Jan. 2007.

Michael Tackett "Richardson in '08 Race," *Chicago Tribune*, Jan. 22, 2007.

Stuart Taylor Jr. "The Great Black-White Hope," *National Journal*, Feb. 3, 2007.

Rebecca Traister "Hillary Is Us," *Salon*, Oct. 16, 2006.

Cynthia Tucker "Lingering Sexism Still Pervades High Levels of Power," *Call & Post*, Jan. 18–24, 2007.

Lynn Yaeger "Skirting the Issues," *The Village Voice*, Mar. 7–13, 2007.

Index